# How to Play

By Amos R. Wells

Author of "How to Study,"

"How to Work," etc.

*First Fruits Press*
*Wilmore, Kentucky*
*c2015*

*How to play*, by Amos R. Wells.

First Fruits Press, ©2015
Previously published: Boston and Chicago: United Society of Christian Endeavor, ©1900.

ISBN: 9781621714231 (print), 9781621714248 (digital)

Digital version at http://place.asburyseminary.edu/christianendeavorbooks/10/

First Fruits Press is a digital imprint of the Asbury Theological Seminary, B.L. Fisher Library. Asbury Theological Seminary is the legal owner of the material previously published by the Pentecostal Publishing Co. and reserves the right to release new editions of this material as well as new material produced by Asbury Theological Seminary. Its publications are available for noncommercial and educational uses, such as research, teaching and private study. First Fruits Press has licensed the digital version of this work under the Creative Commons Attribution Noncommercial 3.0 United States License. To view a copy of this license, visit http://creativecommons.org/licenses/by-nc/3.0/us/.

For all other uses, contact:

First Fruits Press
B.L. Fisher Library
Asbury Theological Seminary
204 N. Lexington Ave.
Wilmore, KY 40390
http://place.asburyseminary.edu/firstfruits

---

Wells, Amos R. (Amos Russel), 1862-1933.
   How to play / by Amos R. Wells.
   162 pages ; 21 cm.
   Wilmore, Ky. : First Fruits Press, ©2015.
   Reprint. Previously published: Boston : United Society of Christian Endeavor, ©1900.
   ISBN: 9781621714231 (pbk.)
   1. Play. I. Title.
LB1137 .W44 2015                                            372.216

---

Cover design by Jonathan Ramsay

asburyseminary.edu
800.2ASBURY
204 North Lexington Avenue
Wilmore, Kentucky 40390

First Fruits Press
*The Academic Open Press of Asbury Theological Seminary*
204 N. Lexington Ave., Wilmore, KY 40390
859-858-2236
first.fruits@asburyseminary.edu
asbury.to/firstfruits

# How to Play

# The "How" Series

By Amos R. Wells

How to Play
How to Work
How to Study

# How to Play

By AMOS R. WELLS
*Author of "How to Study," "How to Work," etc.*

United Society of Christian Endeavor
Boston and Chicago

Copyright, 1900,
by the
UNITED SOCIETY OF CHRISTIAN ENDEAVOR

# CONTENTS

| CHAP. | | PAGE |
|---|---|---|
| I. | THE DUTY OF PLAYING | 7 |
| II. | PLAYING BY PROXY | 14 |
| III. | GAMES OF SOLITAIRE | 20 |
| IV. | "NO ONE WILL PLAY WITH ME" | 24 |
| V. | AN APPETITE FOR PLAY | 27 |
| VI. | DROP YOUR WORK | 30 |
| VII. | FUN THAT FITS | 33 |
| VIII. | FLABBY PLAYING | 36 |
| IX. | OVERDOING IT | 42 |
| X. | CANDY, CLOTHES, AND CONSCIENCE | 46 |
| XI. | HOW TO KEEP GAMES FRESH | 49 |
| XII. | A RECREATION SCHEDULE | 52 |
| XIII. | PLAY AND "THE PLAY" | 58 |
| XIV. | TIPSY-TOED RECREATION | 63 |
| XV. | GAMES OF CHANCE | 66 |
| XVI. | PLAYING AT LOVE | 72 |
| XVII. | FUN ALIVE AND FUN DEAD | 77 |
| XVIII. | FUN AFOOT | 79 |
| XIX. | RECREATION ON TWO WHEELS | 83 |
| XX. | OUT IN THE OPEN | 87 |
| XXI. | ESTABLISHING OUR MACKINACS | 90 |
| XXII. | HOW TO SPOIL A VACATION | 95 |
| XXIII. | THE PLEASURES OF THE TONGUE | 99 |
| XXIV. | READING THAT RECREATES | 103 |
| XXV. | WRITING FOR FUN | 112 |
| XXVI. | THE FAMILY ROUND TABLE | 116 |
| XXVII. | THE HOME ORCHESTRA | 119 |
| XXVIII. | SOME HINTS FOR ENTERTAINERS | 122 |
| XXIX. | YOUR OWN GAMES | 130 |
| XXX. | A GAME REPERTOIRE | 133 |

# HOW TO PLAY.

## CHAPTER I.

### THE DUTY OF PLAYING.

I HAD a dog once which, like all young dogs, knew how to play. On sight of me at the farthest distance, he would come flashing out, quivering in every eager muscle, and alive in every burnished hair of his ruddy coat. He tumbled over and over in his extravagance of joy till it almost seemed that the puppy's frantic revolutions had turned him into a globe of frisky fur, belted by that very unsteady equator, his plumed and whirling tail. There was more whole-hearted merriment in a single lithe, barking prance of that young puppy than in many an evening party undertaken by fashionable undertakers; more laughter and good cheer in his jolly bark than in all the jerky giggles ever squeezed out of tight boots or a tight bodice; more of genuine,

renewing sport in his sparkling eyes than ever gleamed palely from above a simpering mustache or darted from under a coquette's pencilled brows.

I used that ecstatic puppy as a sort of character guage. When, at his jovial advances,—a ball of furry sunshine, a barking challenge to the blues to put on gloves with him if they dared,—when, at my young dog's absolutely sincere and delightful approach, skirts were drawn up primly, or broadcloth manifested an uneasy dread of mud, when brows contracted, and lips looked sour, and eyes grew hard and cold,—well, my puppy had found a very unfortunate man, a very pitiable woman. But when, at sight of the onrushing cataract of puppyish jollity, faces were wreathed in cordial smiles, hands came eagerly out of restraining kids, eyes lighted up in roguish sympathy with this bit of God's sunshiny nature, and the whole heart was evidently longing to break through the bondage of broadcloth or silk, of years, or people's opinion, and, as in the blessed childhood, to abandon itself to the puppy's carousal of glee,—then, why then, my young dog had found for me, in nine cases out of ten, a strong, sweet-spirited, tender-hearted, courageous, and blessed man or woman.

I no longer have the use of that animated

character gauge, for my gay dog is dead. But as Carlo became an old dog, as the charms of puppyhood fell from his curly back, as the years brought the sedateness they bring to dogs and men alike, to the dog they brought no souring of the spirit, no grim, prim stiffness of demeanor. His advance was still a tumbling cataract of jollity, tamed but slightly by the rheumatism. Tin cans, small boys, kicking cows could make no havoc of his irrepressible good humor. When disease had plainly settled upon him, he preached me many a sermon by his bounding geniality, so painful to his body that it often ended in a distressful whine and a puzzled look in the brown eyes, as if they really could not understand why muscles should grow old while the spirit is young, and legs be stiffened beneath a dancing heart. And as the old dog came to die, he used his last remaining strength in trying to wag his tail.

I am going to take that puppy, the merry life he lived and the merry death he died, as the text of this book. Solomon sent the world to an invertebrate, to learn how to work by considering the ant. For a model of the more difficult art, the art of right playing, I have had to take, you see, a higher animal, a vertebrate.

Should men become puppies, you ask, and live like creatures of the day, careless of their immortal souls? No, by no means; let us have no more puppies in human form than we have now. But I have never yet discovered why it is necessary to be unhappy and disagreeable because one has a soul. I have never yet found out why it is necessary, in order to learn how to work, to forget how to play. No minister of the good tidings has ever yet undertaken to prove to me the necessity, in order to become like those little children the Master gives us for models, that we should omit from our character the gay light-heartedness which is one of their pre-eminent charms. I never yet could see why, in order to substantiate humanity's claim to be better than the brutes, we need in any particular be worse than they. It is a blessed thing to grow old with a bounding gayety of heart, though not of body, such as my old dog had.

Have you read that sketch by Robert J. Burdette, wherein he describes his feelings as he watched a gay band of young revellers, their hands grasping a string and eagerly sliding to and fro upon it, while an earnest young man in the centre tried to locate the fugitive key? As Burdette noted the intent faces, the bubbling merriment, the happy eyes of that group, jolly representative though he is of the gospel of good cheer, uppermost in his mind was the thought, "What idiocy! Watch those silly hands, sliding inanely back and forth over that simple string!" Then came an alarming discovery: "Bob Burdette, you are growing old. Your heart has lost its youthful simplicity, for such things pleased you, too, once, and now they only disgust." Then came a resolution, which this mirthful philosopher urges upon all that have reached the turning of the tide,—a resolution to share no more in youthful glee to be a dampener of young people's sport. Well, well! I always fancied that it must be a rather serious thing to furnish fun for a continent, but I never thought that the humorist's sad career could so tame a genial heart.

Who has not seen bearded men and matronly women,—yes, and spectacled grandsires, and grandmas with snowy hair beneath their caps, —clamored for by children more than the gayest youthful leader of their games? Men and women that grow old in the right way are always the very life and soul of all meetings of young people. They have been playing so much longer than the youngsters, you see, that they know just how to do it. They have resources in this delightful art of which those young apprentices, apt scholars though they may be, know nothing. God pity the household that has no young-old person in it to teach the boys and girls how to play. The world, bitter and harsh oftentimes, will not fail in precepts of industry; but in default of frolicsome father or mother, or game-loving grandfather or maiden aunt, what a doleful household there will be!

You have watched them grow up, have you not,—these poor little boys and girls that never learned how to play? One would not mind the stiffening of their muscles, though muscles are not made to grow stiff; but how sad to see the stiffening of their manners! One would not mind the wrinkles on the forehead and about the corners of the mouth, though these are not necessary nor handsome; but we sorrow to see the temper become flabby. The slow, tedious gait and constrained movements would vex us little, though men and women have no right thus to disgrace the wonderful mechanism of the body; but we mourn the loss of mental agility and spiritual alacrity.

Have you ever thought what an artist would do to transform a picture of the average infant into a picture of the average person of middle age? He would make the face longer, the nose sharper, the lips thinner, the cheek-bones more prominent, the eyes colder, the skin yellow, the muscles shrunken, the lines angular. To be sure, he would widen the forehead, but might he not widen the forehead without making these other, these lamentable, changes? Must experience bring with it sourness? Need age be less lovely and jubilant than babyhood because it is more learned? Must we sell our hearts to buy our brains, and in our spiritual market reports quote success in terms of happiness? That we may grow old more wisely than the dog, must we grow old more sadly?

The only true Christian is the light-hearted Christian. Sir John Lubbock has two companion essays. One he styles "The Happiness of Duty," the other, "The Duty of Happiness." Joyousness is possible for every Christian, therefore joyousness is obligatory upon every Christian. So rare is really sane sport, that of Sir John's two essays the latter may actually be more important than the former, and it is becoming the duty of one who cares for the welfare of his brothers to place emphasis upon the duty of Christian play, as upon the duty of Christian work.

## CHAPTER II.

### PLAYING BY PROXY.

WHAT a farce is much of our modern play! Have you ever stopped to calculate how much of the sport of the American people is carried on by proxy? A thousand men and boys gather in God's sunshine, surrounded by His inspiring air, with the blood in their veins and the muscles of their bodies. begging for a rough-and-tumble game with the elements; these thousand men and boys troop forth some summer day for sport. What is the sport? To sit on crowded, uncomfortable boards, breathing tobacco smoke, and eating peanuts, and howling, while eighteen men, some score of yards away, are doing their playing for them! Twenty thousand people to watch a game of baseball! What a toughening must have come to those twenty thousand sets of muscles,—through the eyes! How the blood must have been invigorated, and the brain cleared, and foul air driven from the lungs,—through the eyes!

People of the United States do a vast deal of playing by proxy. After a great game of baseball what large editions of our papers are sold, and how many hundreds of dandies, with cigarettes held in their nerveless hands that never felt a baseball bat in their flabby lives, spend their nickels to see whether the Chicagoes or Cincinnatis or Clevelands came out ahead! Better five hours with bat in hand or speeding around the diamond, than a lifetime of newspaper reading about games played by others. Better a day's vigorous pull at the oars than attendance on all the regattas that ever were. Better a ten-mile walk on your own feet, than the witnessing of all the O'Learys and Westons that ever trod the sawdust path. Better a twenty-mile spin on your own bicycle, than all the programmes of all the fancy riders on this planet. Better a thousandfold the clumsiest activity of your own body and brain, than the spectacle of the most proficient amusement-mongers this lazy world ever paid to do its playing for it.

The "playhouse" and the "play,"—what a sarcasm has crept into the English language! Immense buildings by the hundred, all over this great land, crowded nightly with an open-mouthed, staring crowd, who sit for three hours resignedly, while a set of painted and bedizened ladies and gentlemen on the stage do their playing for them. It is hardly thus that the child's dramas are carried on at school recess. Every boy or girl must be on the stage, must be a king or queen, a duke, at least, or there is trouble at once. No spectators there, while other people play!

Now I hope you will not misunderstand me. This is no tirade against championship games or regattas. But let us all have enough common sense to recognize the fact that we are not playing when we merely watch the sport of others, no matter whether we pay a dollar for that privilege or not. And let us not join that throng of weak-eyed, loose-jointed, simpering, lackadaisical men and women, boys and girls, those lazy, conceited, dull-spirited, sickly folks, whose only playing is done by proxy.

I summon you to a life of mirth, to years filled with the exuberant joy of physical exercise in manly and womanly sports, to years bright with games and all innocent recreations. My business brings me into yearly contact with crowds of young people, hundreds of whom make the mistake of thinking that time taken for play is just so much robbed from work, and time robbed from play just so much clear gain for industry. They think that if steady application is a good thing, continual application must be a better thing. They believe that if four hours are spent on a lesson instead of two hours, the lesson will be learned twice as well. Conceding that all work and no play makes Jack a dull boy, they claim that they are geniuses and not Jacks; and dozens of them are victims of that unworded popular belief, that they are playing when they are only watching other people play. Then I have watched them after they leave school (this sort is rarely graduated), and I have yet to see one such student rise above mediocrity, nor do I expect ever to see such a prodigy. How could it be ? In this rushing, busy world, how should a man succeed in his work, or a woman in hers, who has not learned to play ?

Why, success nowadays absolutely demands a healthy body. They used to make out of the sickly son a preacher or a college professor. The days are past when such a disposition was possible. The demands made now on men and women of all callings are so strenuous that an invalid or a semi-invalid is drawn aside from the race almost before the word "Go." And health is impossible for any long time to any one who has not an abnormally strong constitution, without some active and cheerful sport.

Besides health, success also demands push,

vivacity, energy. No man can succeed in the most humble work without will power. Other ages have been ages of gold or iron or bronze; but this is the age of steam, and not merely of boiling water, but of what Paul calls "boiling spirit"; "fervent in spirit," our translation reads. Cold-blooded men and women must fall to the rear. Men and women of ready adaptability, of quick and keen perceptions, of vim and vigor,—the demand of our times has wrought out the needed supply of these. Now the man who has forgotten how to play is a man half-asleep. He is in a semi-torpid condition. Sport, mirth, recreation, are absolutely necessary to maintain an alert brain, a wide-awake set of powers.

But, most of all, success in these times requires a cheery and serene nature. You think that a queer statement, having doubtless in your mind some fussy, worrying rich man of your acquaintance. But none the less the statement is true, and I repeat it, that the men in any honorable calling who achieve a permanent, worthy success are men who at regular and frequent intervals escape from the tension, the fume, the toil, of their business, to make themselves over fresh and new, re-create themselves, that is, with hearty, innocent mirth. At a time when nervous disorders are becoming alarmingly prevalent, and sudden deaths of overworked men startlingly frequent, material for the support of my declaration is sure to be plentiful within the circle of each man's acquaintance; and I have no doubt that your own experience and observation will show you that when other things are equal, it is always the man of equanimity, of peaceful serenity, of a gay and mirthful temper, who bears life's stress most victoriously, and lasts the longest to accomplish the most. It is because play produces health, vivacity, and serenity that I make for it the claim that it is one of the essentials to a successful career in these days. Not playing by proxy, however; not playing by proxy.

## CHAPTER III.

#### GAMES OF SOLITAIRE.

ALL games of cards are about equally inane, but one game caps the climax of absurdity, the game of solitaire. To sit down in a corner by one's self, and at the dictate of chance, with a modicum of skill, transfer bits of pasteboard from one heap to another,—that is an idiotic occupation. But many men who do not play cards really transform their amusements into games of solitaire. A newspaper or a novel read while the whole family is mute that the one may enjoy it, a walk or a ride brooding gloomily alone, a bit of fancy work in one's own room, a poem or a story scribbled in privacy, received in stricter privacy on its sure return from the dread sanctum, and burned in strictest privacy of all,—those are some of the games of solitaire in which men and women, young and old, often indulge.

Whatever the sport, comradeship is essential to its success as a recreation. No sport can take a man out of himself when he is by himself. A friend will count your worries an impertinence, and you will resent the introduction of his, and thus you will be mutually beneficial.

Then, too, if you are to become enthusiastic in your play, you need the spur of competition. Two will walk farther than one; two will read more than one; two will become more expert hunters or fishers than one; two will find more beauties in Shakespeare or Browning than one. Where one sees monotony, two will develop variety. Where one loses interest, two will constantly gain enthusiasm.

This is the age of co-operation, of co-working. It must become the age of co-playing, too, before all is well. Division of labor is a valuable method, but so, too, is division of play. Labor unions are becoming a feature of our civilization; play unions must follow, are following. We have Knights of Labor; we must also enroll ourselves among the Knights of Play. It is a glorious sign of progress in these latest decades that men are banding together, not only for making money in trade, and for defence in government, and for philanthropy in churches, but for good cheer and jovial brotherhood in many social organizations. The Chautauqua Circles, the University Extension movement, the Browning clubs, the chess clubs,—those are samples of the modern methods of mental recreation. The baseball clubs, bicycle clubs, turnvereins, Y. M. C. A. gymnasiums, tennis clubs, clubs for yachting, canoeing, lacrosse, football,—those are samples of modern methods of physical recreation. Form a club, then, I say; not "A Club of One," as that bright little grunting book has it, but a club of two at least,—you and a congenial friend.

Remember in this co-operative—or, rather, co-recreative—company that all such unions, to be effective, must be based on compromises. Everything worth having has its price, and the price of the inspiration and pleasure of a friend's companionship in your sports is occasional yielding to that friend's whims and wishes, study of his bent as well as of your own, and sympathy with his varying moods. Recreation is mainly to get away from one's self awhile, that God may have a chance at that self and strengthen it without our blundering interference. Therefore, recreation must be unselfish.

But there is yet more to this matter. Most young men and women are anxious to make a good appearance before their fellows, to be brilliant members of society, as the phrase goes. That accomplishment, though possible to any young lady by nature's favoritism, is possible for a young man only as he has won for himself this glad gift of playing. Not by any means that social intercourse is all play, or that a man must not have solidly valuable parts in order to shine before his fellows; but, none the less, a man cannot be popular in society, and does not deserve to be, that has not become able to sympathize fully and lovingly with others, to drop his selfish worries in their presence, to avoid forcing his toil unduly upon them, and to take kindly interest in their plans for pleasure and for labor. This power of self-forgetfulness and abandonment is to be learned only through play. A man who is too much absorbed in his business to throw it aside occasionally for a pleasant chat with a friend, for a game or walk or ride, is too much absorbed in himself to make a popular member of that club of self-effacement called society. Therefore this recreation rule, Have comradeship in your sports and learn to be unselfish in them, has wider range than appears at first.

## CHAPTER IV.

### "NO ONE WILL PLAY WITH ME."

BELIEVE, therefore, in comradeship in sport, and I am a born foe to self-centred recreation. A game is to take a man out of himself, to get him away from his worries; and the more of himself and the less of other people there is in it, the less recreative value will it have for him.

Not always, however, is it possible to find a companion for one's sport, and so it becomes a necessary, though not by any means the most pleasing, branch of the player's art to learn how to play by himself.

A baby knows how to do it. Every pink toe is a separate comrade. What fascinating fun lies hidden in his rattle! And if neither toe nor rattle is available, then, colic permitting, there is a whole theatre of amusement in a sunbeam, or a blue globe over the gas-jet.

I still preserve, as a standing object-lesson to my less resourceful maturity, the big box of spools wherewith I played for hours at a time, all by myself, when I was a boy. The No. 40's were generals, I remember, the No. 80's were privates, and the gradation was properly made between the two. This big purple one was a king. What dress parades! What battles, with marbles for cannon-balls! What gorgeous court ceremonials! I remember that when I read "The Conquest of Granada," every detail of that picturesque history was faithfully wrought out with my spools. What would I not give if those spools meant as much to me now!

For the time came when I wanted "some one to play with me," when I could not think of anything to do, when I wandered uneasily from cellar to garret, begging now this one and now that to have a game of croquet, or go and catch butterflies, or play parchesi with me. And when no one could do it, or would do it, I was miserable. I have seen grown men and women in just that predicament.

Now this should be one of the gains of recreation, that it renders the player independent. It should give him a mental poise that enables him to stand alone, to be sufficient unto himself. No one, therefore, should permit himself to become solely attached to any form of recreation that requires a comrade—such as tennis, or chess. Every one should add to his recreation outfit some amusement he can readily enjoy in solitude—the reading of books, the writing of poetry, canoeing, bicycling, walking. And though he will, of course, engage a friend with himself in his sport whenever he can, he will keep himself in the practice of solitude by an occasional stroll or ride or row without a companion. He will become lord of his mind and his moods, and he will be a cheery and satisfactory comrade for himself.

How serviceable this faculty is, no one will realize until life's troubles come, and the hardnesses of one's own lot, or the sins and selfishness of others shut one in to loneliness. It is worth to a man or a woman all the wealth of the world to possess inner and independent resources, to be able to play by one's self, to win and hold a strong body and a serene spirit, though all mankind may go a different way.

## CHAPTER V.

### AN APPETITE FOR PLAY.

IT is better to eat from compulsion than to starve to death, but food does very little good until we eat with an appetite. There is a time for all things, a time to work and a time to play, and the best time to play is when work is ended. There may, of course, be conditions so adverse to recreation that sport must be had in the midst of working hours or not at all, but usually sport is as much a failure when sandwiched in among work as would be a slice of custard pie between two layers of beef. To sport which is to be successful must be brought a clear conscience and a relieved sense of duty done. One cannot re-create what has not been dis-created.

Of course this is why the playing of so many people of wealth and fashion is such a dismal farce, just as are their dinners. There is no appetite for either. Indeed, they consider an appetite quite a vulgar and plebeian thing. An appetite is born of wasted tissues, crying out for repair. And those whose life is like the butterflies' can no more play than the butterfly can. Who ever saw a jolly butterfly, a butterfly on a lark, a butterfly that looked as if it were laughing? And so the poor rich people who do not have to work are obliged to invent all sorts of make-believe tasks, bogus labor, to cheat themselves into the belief that they are tired and add spice to their dismal recreation. No. Let us who belong to the only happy class, whether rich or poor, the working class,—let us know that sport comes best which comes to tired nerves and worn-out muscles and depressed spirits, but which comes to set its crown of revivifying sunshine upon work accomplished and difficulties victoriously surmounted.

It is a happy thing to be able to drop work and worries in the midst, to leap to the playground, gather up wide armfuls of refreshment, and spring back to toil again, a giant with vigor redoubled by the touch of earth; but it is a far happier thing to be able by energy and will to push the tasks to a conclusion before the hour for sport arrives, for play makes fine battlements to a day, but a poor foundation or middle course.

And furthermore, if you wish to have an appetite for the next playtime when it arrives, learn to stop your play while your interest in it is at its height. It is the one game too much that transforms a sport into a bore. It is the last half mile after you get tired that spoils bicycle-riding for you. It is the "just one more song" after your throat has become weary that ruins your voice and your pleasure.

The wise doctors tell us that if we wish to digest our food well and come up to every meal with that keen-edged appetite which does so much to hew one's way through life, we must always stop eating just before we are quite satisfied. If you have dyspepsia, that piece of advice is alone worth more than the price of this book. The same good rule applies to recreation: stop with an appetite for more; never permit yourself to reach the vulgar and mischievous moment of repletion.

## CHAPTER VI.

#### DROP YOUR WORK.

MANY bring into their recreation hours so many burdens from their working hours that their sport is only half sport. They try to play leap-frog with a bundle of unlearned lessons astride their back. Their tennis racket is weighted down with unanswered letters. Their bicycle joints are rusty with unmet engagements. The bright story they are reading to relieve the mind from business worries is black with them on every page.

Recreation can never be re-creation thus. As well might the consumptive box up the air of his sick-room and carry it to Colorado with him. If you meet in the road a barrier over which you must leap, you run back half a dozen yards to get a fresh start. But your running back will do very little good if you carry the barrier with you. Recreation is to get this fresh start, and if we are not silly enough to carry our obstacles with us to our sport, when we come up again after our half-dozen yards of recession, all fresh and eager for the leap, we go with ease over a fence that seemed stupendous before, or often find the fence miraculously sunk out of the way entirely.

"Well," you say, "that's all right in theory, but in practice it's very hard to drop one's work and one's worries." You tell me that my metaphor is wrong, that these worries are not things that we carry at our will and drop when we please, but sticky things that adhere and things with hooks well barbed that cling and will not let loose. There is much truth in this, because none of us is complete master of his mind. Yet it is possible so to drill ourselves to play that when the time comes for the renewing hour we shall strip off for it every trouble and vexation of spirit, as a small boy denudes himself for a jolly plunge in the pond.

It is partly a matter of temperament, but it is chiefly a matter of will. If a man may have "a will to work," why may he not also have "a will to play"? We often hear it said, by work-drunkards, that they have no appetite for play. All games seem insipid, childish; they cannot "get up an interest" in any recreation. But one of the commonest experiences of workers is to begin on a distasteful task, force the mind to diligent application, and emerge from the toil not only triumphant, but actually longing for more of the same work to do. Laboring at first from a sense of duty, they came to labor from pleasure.

It is the same way with playing; and though sport is a poor kind of sport when we "make a business of it," yet for many men no other entrance to the delights of recreation is open to their toil-hardened hearts. At first, certainly, and possibly forever, they must take their amusements sadly, as the English are said to do.

The same stern quality of mind that enables a worker to cast aside his play and all thoughts of it when he enters his workshop, will enable him, when he drags his unwilling soul to the playground, decisively to abandon his toil. Both work and play are spoiled if this is not done; and important as it is to concentrate the mind on one's task, I certainly would not call it a less important matter to concentrate the mind on one's play.

## CHAPTER VII.

### FUN THAT FITS.

NO slight factor in the high art of recreation consists in fitting the game to the man. Choose some sport in which you can excel, and get up a pride in your proficiency. If chess, my young carpenter, is your recreation, become a first-class chess-player. Buy your Staunton and study up, and be prepared to floor every champion in town. If carpentering is your recreation, my dear doctor, make accurate joints and clear-cut edges and turn out jobs to which you can point with complacency. If you go into walking or running, my pale-faced student, win to yourself such calves that you can annihilate space, and do your forty miles a day to the admiration of all beholders. Thus only can you banish care from your sport, by getting up a counter-interest, by setting up an opposing attraction.

Now I do not mean that you are to become cranks and ride hobbies. I do not mean that your whole life is to model itself to fit the baseball diamond, or become checkered with the chess-board squares. I do not mean that all your interests are to revolve about the bicycle hub, or to hang from your fishing-rod. Not at all. Professionalism, or even an approach to it, is death to all right playing. Sport is at an end when sport is made the end of sport. You have no business to make a business of playing. Life is not for sport, but sport is for life, and so you must put life into it; that is all. Make it the main object of your life, my young clerk in the drug-store, to play finely on the fiddle, and the main object of your fiddle-playing is destroyed. Count success in story-writing, my young mechanic, your chief good, and the chief good of story-writing for you is a failure. Yet none the less, though this peril lurks in waiting and must be shunned,—none the less it is true that sport to be profitable must be absorbing and enthusiastic, and to be enthusiastic must be something of which we can be proud.

I would not advise a fat old merchant, for instance, to take up football for his amusement. He had better join a bowling club. I would not advise a weary schoolma'am, on her feet all day, to buy a bicycle. She had better loaf in the woods with Gray's " Manual of Botany," and become an oracle on flowers. I would not advise a tired-out farmer's boy, stiff from the plough-handles and disgusted with the very thought of out-of-doors or of plants, to buy a botany, but I would set him to reading Sir Walter Scott.

I, being kept indoors eight hours at a stretch, must find my sport outside the house; and, since Nature has made me long and fashioned me after the model of a pair of compasses, I find the chief solace of my life in walking. But if I should meet an elephant of a man, short-winded and weak-kneed, I should not expect him to enjoy walking just because I do. Nature never intended him for a space-annihilator.

So let us choose sports with an eye to a fair degree of excellence in them, and determine to become enthusiastic in the matter, that our joy in them may banish cares and worries for one brief hour, at least.

## CHAPTER VIII.

#### FLABBY PLAYING.

ONE of life's most annoying and disheartening experiences is to try to amuse a listless, lackadaisical person, who says, when you ask him whether he would like to play some game, "O, I don't care"; and who says, when you ask him *what* he would like to play, "O, I don't ca-are"; and who says, when you ask him whether he would like another game, "O, I don't ca-a-a-are"; who has to be told always when it is his turn; who never has any idea how the score stands; who is all the time whining about the game's being so hard, or the weather's being so hot; who, at the crisis of the game, begins to talk about the last novel; who stifles a yawn in the midst of your explanations of the sport, and goes through the whole performance with the air of a martyr. One might ask why such persons ever play at all, but the reason is easy: if they had grit enough to say they didn't want to play, they would have grit enough to play well and to enjoy playing.

No profit comes from the sluggish entering into any amusement. If it will not stir your blood and your brain, if it will not kindle your eye and give your voice a new ring, you might as well be lying on your back snoring as playing tennis or crokinole or golf. Games are to take us out of ourselves, to bury our worries in their excitement, to turn our interest into new channels. Sport is like a carriage rolling us swiftly into fresh scenes; but there are some people that will not give themselves up to the carriage. They sit with every muscle tense, grimly upright, and doing two hours' work in riding ten miles.

The secret of successful work lies quite as much in the letting go as in the taking hold. Men whose work is ever with them do not amount to much at the work. If you are unable to throw yourself heartily into your recreation, I do not believe you can throw yourself heartily into your occupation. You are not your own master to do what you will with yourself, but your work has become your master. It is a poor preacher who insists on preaching to you his next sermon while out for a bicycle ride. It is a second-rate merchant that must always talk shop. The men whose noses are forever on the grindstone soon wear down not only their noses, but their brains.

The essence of walking is *fast* walking. The essence of bowling is " spares " and " strikes " and a big yell every time one is achieved. The essence of quoits is " leaners " and " ringers " and exultation thereupon. The essence of dominoes is " to domino," and to paint things red when you have done it. In fine, the essence of any sport is to go into it all over and not merely touch it with your finger-tips, to rejoice in it, crow over it, frisk and gambol through it, and be a boy or a girl again.

Let no one understand me as teaching that the chief end of a game is to beat. I have learned much about playing by attending the university presided over by my small daughter, Caroline. She was a long time in grasping the idea of a game. With her, as doubtless with most children, the first game was hide-and-seek, but it was a very primitive hide-and-seek. I would solemnly put my hands over my eyes, and away would dart the midget to the other side of the room, where she would possibly bury her head in the sofa pillows. " Hoo-o-oo ! " she would cry, and I, turning my back upon her, would hunt behind doors, under chairs, beneath the table-spread. Her bright eye would be on my operations, I was sure, for every failure was met with a delighted giggle. A very little of this sufficed, however, for my impatient girlie.

"Hee' yi!" ("Here am I!") the wee voice would pipe out, and she would fling herself upon me in a torrent of bubbling laughter. Ah, it was a fascinating game.

There was not half the fun when *I* hid, because, in my stupid, grown-up way of doing things, I would a find *real* hiding-place. I would often go so far as to get behind the door or under the piano, and very soon I would hear a little girl breathing hard, and a pleading cry on the edge of a sob would warn me to rush from my ambush and begin to play again.

Caroline was right, as usual, and the tiresome folks that play "to beat" are wrong. The heart of a game is not the score, but the merriment; not to be victorious, but to be vivacious; not to beat, but to romp. These solemn-eyed, long-faced ninnies that make an evening's hard, strenuous labor of a game of chess, and worry over their golf record as if it were to go on the books of the recording angel, ought to take a few lessons from Professor Caroline.

I like to watch the children of the slums at their play. They may be hungry half the time, poor little things! but their laugh is as merry as any I ever hear on Commonwealth Avenue or Beacon Street, and their play is heartier. Their manners, too, will not suffer much in the comparison.

One day I sat in Copps Hill Burying-ground, Boston, rejoicing in the cool shadows, lazily reading the inscriptions on the antique gravestones that were wagging their weary heads around me, and wondering, as I looked over the beautiful waters at Charlestown and Bunker Hill across the way, whether General Gage ever came back from the spirit land to visit again the spot from which he bombarded and fired Charlestown so many decades ago.

I was considering thoughtfully a very sad tombstone which set forth the death of four children, each of whom passed away before the first twelvemonth had gone by, when my attention was attracted to six children of modern Boston. In that crowded portion of the slums the graveyard must be utilized as a park, and the little Jewish and Italian children are given free range over the ancient sepulchres. There was a drinking-fountain near me, and three boys and three girls were having much sport there. I watched them.

The smallest boy—so small that he could scarcely reach the basin—had part of an old toy cornet, and he was filling its battered brass tube with water. Then he put one end in his mouth, and blew with all his might. The water rushed out through the curved tube and struck him full in the face. At this the urchin and all his comrades capered around, their bare feet twinkling, their voices high in a cackle of delight. The oldest girl was especially tickled. "Let me! Let me!" she cried, snatching the magic instrument. "P—ff!" and her own face was splashed all over with the cool water. "Ha, ha, ha, ha—a!" and she doubled up, her hands on her sides, in a very paroxysm of glee. And then they must all have a turn. And then they must all do it over again. And then they must try—though not very successfully—to turn the twisted tube on one another. Fun? If they have such fun on Commonwealth Avenue or Beacon Street, the urchins keep it decidedly to themselves.

This pretty little scene will stick in my mind as a type of the right kind of sport. It is so much better to throw water in one's own face than beer or whiskey or tobacco smoke or salacious novels. It is so much better to dabble in God's fountains than in the "pool" of the gambler. It was so much better even to wet their clothes that hot July day than to water stocks. And those six children of the slums, in their madcap silliness around that graveyard fountain, were in so much better business than most that would look down upon them from out of their coach and fours!

## CHAPTER IX.

#### OVERDOING IT.

WHEN Paderewski came to Boston, the long-haired musician attracted throngs limited only by the size of the hall. The tickets were to be sold on Monday morning, beginning at nine o'clock. On *Saturday afternoon* at three, the crowd of would-be buyers began to gather. There they waited, in most dismal quarters, all Saturday night, all Sunday, all Sunday night, and triumphantly led the assault on the box-office Monday morning. Women almost fainted away. Some of them had books to read. Some sat on the floor. Many had fortified themselves with lunches. Others had friends who beguiled the tedium. Of course, those that endured the longest wait were the speculators, who were not there merely for fun; but still there were many who, through no other motive than pleasure-seeking, spent many hours in that dreary corridor.

Now I am no heathen. I have heard Paderewski, and I should like to hear him again.

I trust I am not altogether insensible to the charms and the value of music. And yet when I hear and see such exhibitions as this, I cannot help asking myself: "What view of life have these people? What idea of eternity? What conception of the issues of our existence, of the need of the world or the responsibility of life?" To sit on the floor ten hours—nay, a single hour—at the feet of any man, no matter how long his hair, how angelic his smile, or how nimble his fingers, comes pretty close to heathenish idolatry.

Recreation loses all its value, and becomes instantly a *dis*-creation, as soon as a man or a woman ceases to be its master and becomes its slave. It is bad enough when what should be one's avocation practically supercedes his vocation; but when his recreation supplants both vocation and avocation, alas for that life! When the teacher subordinates his teaching to his tennis, and the preacher is evidently less enthusiastic for the gospel than for golf, the sport that should have made more of a worker has made less of a worker, and through this overdoing the player is undone.

Does a man realize what he has gained in attaining the distinction so many are anxious to attain, in being called a "sport"? It means that he has merged his identity in his amusement. He is no more Harry Heady, but a "crank" to turn a bicycle. She is no more Susy Sweetzer, but a "stick" to propel a golf ball. The means has become the end, the machine takes the place of the product, and recreation, whose office is to restore energy and invigorate the mind, becomes a spendthrift of energy and the goal of all the thoughts. Intelligence, that should have leaped from the wide landscape with renewed zest to the work of life, continues to whirl around with the bicycle wheel; the man has "wheels in his head."

This is the chief reason why it is best to know and come to enjoy a great variety of amusements, such as this book indicates. Those that over-play are almost always attached to some one game or sport. It is an excellent plan, if your reason tells you that you are growing too fond of canoeing, resolutely to drop the paddle for a time and take up the tennis racket. If chess has become a time-eating hobby, stable the horse, knight and all, and prove your manhood on crokinole.

The safety test is this: While you look forward to the sport with pleasure and engage in it zealously, can you forget it absolutely when worktime comes? It is necessary to drop work completely if one is really to play, but it is necessary to drop play completely if one is to get good from it. It is a question of the transformation of forces. Here is the sunshine, building itself up through long, bright hours into the fuel, into the hickory wood. Now what is to become of the wood? Is it to rot on the ground where it grew? or is it to warm our workrooms and drive our engines? That is the question. According to the answer, play is a blessing or a bane.

## CHAPTER X.

#### CANDY, CLOTHES, AND CONSCIENCE.

NOW I can close my list of requirements for the best playing with a queer trio; namely, these: No recreation can be a success that is not based upon sensible eating, sensible dressing, and a good conscience.

No one can play when he has a headache or a toothache, dyspepsia or biliousness. The nations—did you ever think of it?—that best know how to play, best know how to eat, eat fewest sweetmeats and most of food for bone and blood and brain, eat less for the doctors, the confectioners, the bakers, drink less for the brewers, the distillers, and soda-water men, and eat and drink more for character, for manliness and womanliness.

I have seen, first and last, a great many schoolgirls and schoolboys who sinned in this regard, who, with little exaggeration, breakfasted on bananas and chocolate, dined on pie and coffee, and lunched on cake, candy, and tea. In running over the list in my mind, I do not find one who was not a languid, lank, lackadaisical specimen of boyhood or girlhood, totally incapable of a genuine laugh, and ignorant of the meaning of a game. I have knowledge, too, of many a business man whose breakfast is fifty hurried gulps of hot cakes and strong coffee, whose lunch is coffee again and a piece of mince pie, and whose dinner is the rest of the bill of fare. Cross? Of course they are. And the evening backgammon or a "sing" before bedtime? As soon expect a hippopotamus to play Chopin. No; bad digestion means bad humor. Bread and meat, milk and fruits,—these make the flashing eye; these are the components of the merriest and lightest laughter; these, to speak in true parable, are the strong horses that draw the chariot of good cheer.

Then as to dress. It is said, you know, that it takes nine tailors to make one man. The tailors and tailoresses have been taking constant and terrible revenge for this maxim by unmaking all the men and women they can lay their tape-measures on. Have you ever seen the tailor-made young man and the tailor-made young woman try to run? A lad or a lass should run as lightly and gracefully as a bird lilts through the air. Let us make a rubber coat that would just fit a swallow and put it on an eagle; let us hang his wings with silk and broadcloth and set the king of birds to soaring. He will not cut as ridiculous a figure as do our tight-booted, tight-waisted, distorted, short-breathed, large-veined, over-weighted, clothes-tortured young men and women when they attempt any out-of-door amusement. If talking about dress, especially feminine dress, ever did any good, I should be tempted to pursue this subject further. Suffice it to say that I will admit no one among my joyous Knights of Play who cannot breathe to the very bottom of the lungs, push blood to the most distant capillary, and show a foot with parallel toes.

The final requisite is a good conscience. I will not dilate upon this head, lest you should dub this a sermon, but will merely say that a harsh word can change the jolliest amusement into labored drudgery, that unfairness destroys whatever peace of mind recreation forms, that spite or anger or bitterness of soul is poison potent enough to blot all good cheer from any life.

## CHAPTER XI.

#### HOW TO KEEP GAMES FRESH.

SUPPOSE you have all noticed—those of you, that is, who are sensible enough to play games—that games are likely to "wear out." Really it is we that wear out, our interest in them being lost. And if one knows how to keep his interest in his sports perennial, he has one of the most important secrets of sane and health-giving amusement.

In the first place, don't make a hobby of any game. Be temperate in all things. Halma comes in, and at once halma is everywhere. We have halma parties, and progressive halma, and what not. Before long, halma is "played out" and thrown away, and a capital game, that should be a permanent possession of our recreation hours, has been spoiled for us. It's like eating candy. Some folks make themselves sick on it, and never want to see a piece of candy again. That is as silly with games as with candy.

In the second place, know a large number of

games, and mix them up. Learn chess, for your more thoughtful hours, when body and not brain is weary. Learn tiddledy-winks and crokinole, to play when brain is weary and you need a game that will not fatigue that castle of the nerves. Get a fund of word games—like lawyer, and proverbs, and logomachy, and spello, and progressive spelling, and anagrams, and how, where, and when, and beast, bird, and fish, and crambo, and capping verses—to play in the twilight. Get games for large parties and games for small groups, rollicking games and sedate games, games historical, biographical, classical, biblical, geographical, scientific, and nonsensical. Become a collector of games, a game student, and always be ready to bring forth from your treasury games new and old. Then games will not grow stale with you.

In the third place, be ingenious to invent variations of games. For instance, the interest in halma was indefinitely prolonged in my own household by instituting the change of placing all the men at the start in two facing phalanxes at the centre; checkers alternates in favor with pyramid checkers; backgammon, with Russian backgammon; and the like.

Fourthly, keep track of your games. Many a game drops out of our lives just because it has been forgotten. We play it at a friend's house and exclaim, "Why, I must get out my old set of dominoes! I had forgotten it was such fun!" Make a list of the games you have and know. Be zealous to enlarge the list. Keep the book handy for reference. I have indicated in a later chapter how you may classify your entries, as "Games for large parties," "Memory games," "Word games," "Catches," "Board games," and the like. This book you may call your recreation ledger, and it will mean for you and yours a growing balance in the Bank of Good Cheer.

And finally, but most important, keep your games fresh by bringing in fresh participants. A neighbor's family, invited over for the evening, will freshen up your games most delightfully. A lonely young man, lost in the desert of a boarding-house, will revive your games and be himself revived. Games, like men, must not live to themselves or to their owners.

## CHAPTER XII.

#### A RECREATION SCHEDULE.

PLAY should be planned for, as well as work. A man whose plans for the day leave out recreation is like a steam engine with the safety-valve omitted, except that the explosion of the steam engine is not likely to be so sad and calamitous as is the collapse of the man.

The business-like maxim, "A place for everything, and everything in its place," is applicable to few matters more than to amusements. It is certainly necessary to keep them in their proper place, but it is just as necessary to have a place for them. I don't know which is worse,—to allow them to struggle carelessly over all one's days, or to shut them out of our lives altogether; probably the latter.

That old Russian count, Leo Tolstoi, claims that the twenty-four hours should be thus divided: one-third for sleep, one-third for work, one-third for recreation. And this belief of his he puts into practice. Eight hours for recreation! How many business men do you know, from the cashboy to the president of the railroad company, who take as many minutes? Yet the old count is right, and the best experience of the world, wherever the experiment has been tried, proves that eight hours of work, with the rest of the time for the rebuilding of wasted body and mind, accomplish tasks as great in amount as does our present high-pressure system, and finer far in quality. Of course there will always be social arithmeticians who will be ready to demonstrate that eight hours cannot be equal to twelve. This class of people would want the sun above the horizon all the time, that their crops may grow twice as fast. The mathematicians forget that the crops would be burned up.

I have questioned scores of young men on this matter, and I have yet to find one who, no matter what his employment or how long he worked, could not accomplish more with regular recreation than without it. But it is not always easy to find time for it. The student is hard pressed by angry teachers, and those teachers by the demon of books; the clerk by strict employers, and those employers by a selfish public, which insists on transacting through sixteen hours the business that might as well be transacted in eight. Upon the life of every man or woman, and even upon the life of every boy or girl not very far among the teens, so many duties press that playtime must be planned for if it is to be had at all.

But determine to have it; if not two hours, one; if not one, thirty minutes, or fifteen,— some breathing-spell, regular, certain, full, and free. If it be at the cost of a few dollars, it will save many a doctor's bill. If it lose you certain trade advantages, it will in the end gain vastly more. If your studies must be fewer, or less thorough, you will know more at the end. A living dog is better than a dead lion.

Having planned for your playtime, be inflexible about it. Permit no rush of work to crowd upon it. Every tendency of the times is toward inflexible periods of work and away from certain and sure periods of play. One is no more necessary than the other. Money, business, conscience diseased with a false sense of duty, pressure of competition, interest in your work, a thousand things, will seek to wrest from you your hour of health, of relaxation, of power-getting. Yield not a minute.

I am not certain that it is wise to lay down an order for every day. Our schedule easily becomes our master, and when some task comes along that is not down upon it, some unexpected appeal for our services that is more important than all our other duties put together, it is denied, because it has not been arranged for. Besides, we miss much of the charm of living if we portion off our years too primly into squares and rectangles. We get the cabbage-patch, but we leave out the woodland thicket; and both are needed.

Some schedule, however, is necessary, or nothing will get done, and if we are stout enough not to be dominated by our " best laid schemes," we shall find the schedule an indispensable element of success and happiness.

Many people, if they do not set apart a regular time for play, will never play at all. They are the over-busy folks, the folks that can do all sorts of things, and so have all sorts of things to do, from directing other people's invitations, because they write a nice hand, to presiding at dinners, because they have a witty tongue. (That, forsooth, is anything but recreation!) Or they are sluggish folks, the heavy, ponderous folks, the procrastinating folks that are always thinking that they would like to do something—tomorrow. If such people do not set aside a time for sport, and hold themselves rigorously to it, their stupid days will drag themselves monotonously on, and they will die at last, as so many thousands do die—of stagnation.

An amusement schedule, it must also be noted, greatly increases the pleasure to be obtained from the sport by adding to it the joy of expectation. One goes to bed with more alacrity, thinking of the regular bicycle ride in store for him come sunrise. One gets through his morning tasks with better grace, because there stretches before his vision the daily noon walk, swinging briskly along over country lanes or city boulevards. And all the afternoon moves with speedy pace, because after the tea-things are put away, and the house is tidied for the night, Dorothy and you will sit merrily down for the evening game of checkers. I have known two business men to meet for years on the same suburban train, take out the same pocket chess-board, and settle themselves to a game—taken up where it was left on the preceding day. "Your move, John." "I thought of a winning stroke last night, Sam." How much better that than the solitary, eye-racking newspaper! And I have known a group of gentlemen, one of them, at least, past seventy, who for years left that same train three miles out of the city, and, scorning further aid from steam and steel, trudged gaily office-ward through snow or rain or sunshine. That is what I mean when I talk about playing by schedule; and if your life train has been running without this kind of "half-hour for refreshments," I beg of you at once to alter the time-table.

## CHAPTER XIII.

#### PLAY AND "THE PLAY."

AM tired.

Tired of a great many things, but especially tired of hearing and answering questions about the so-called "doubtful amusements."

"Should a Christian play cards?" "May not a Christian dance—just a little?" "Won't you let us go to the theatre with a clear conscience, if we will be careful to select only proper plays?"

Don't you see, young people, that such questions answer themselves? You don't need to ask me or any one else whether you shall play crokinole, or whether you shall ride the bicycle, or whether you shall go to hear Professor Bright lecture. You ask me about card-playing, dancing, and theatre-going because the all but universal Christian conscience has condemned those amusements, because they are under the ban of Christian sentiment, and you want my say-so to bolster up your uneasy consciences.

Now there is no duty urging you to do any of these things,—nothing but your inclination. On the other hand, the vast majority of Christians advise you not to do them. Conscience is all on one side. This being the case, I could afford to grant that these three amusements are perfectly proper, and yet have the very best of reasons for urging you to let them alone, namely, respect for the opinion of the great body of our Lord's children.

Of course I do not propose to take it for granted that these amusements *are* harmless, but there is absolutely no need to enter into that argument at all. This other argument should be conclusive.

But what a low standard of Christian living is indicated by such questions! Do you suppose Paul, when the Vision stopped him on the way to Damascus, thought twice before he asked, "Lord, what wilt thou have me to do?" and asked first this other question, "Lord, if I become thy disciple, may I still go to the games in the circus?" Do you suppose John, when the Master bade him leave all and follow Him, replied, "Yes, on condition that I may still join now and then in a village dance"?

The truth of the matter is that when one has really become a lover of Christ, loving Him with heart and mind and strength and soul, filled with a sense of eternity, with a passion for the winning of souls,—he is ransomed henceforth from such petty concerns as a pack of cards, or a shaking of feet to a fiddle, or a procession of painted women on the stage. His meat and his drink henceforth, his absorbing pleasure, is to do the will of his Father.

Not that he will not play. Indeed, no one plays better than a Christian, knows more games, and jollier ones. The world is full of them—games as far superior to cards, dancing, and the theatre as the light of the blessed sun is better than gaslight. But even as Paul said, "If meat make my brother to offend, I will eat no flesh while the world standeth"— so the Christian will have nothing to do with doubtful amusements, or doubtful books, or doubtful customs, or doubtful drinks, or doubtful anything else, while there is any doubt about them, while there is in them any possibility of hurting a single soul of those that Christ gave up His life to save.

And now a word more particularly about the theatre, leaving to the following chapters just a word—they deserve no more—about the other principal "doubtful amusements."

The other day I was reading an interesting article by Dr. Charles H. Parkhurst. In this article the famous preacher and reformer says

## PLAY AND "THE PLAY." 61

that he believes profoundly in the theatre, and holds that "as a means of intellectual stimulus and of moral uplift there is nothing, with the possible exception of the pulpit, that could stand alongside of it as an enginery of personal effect, provided only it would maintain itself in its proper character as the dramatized incarnation of strength."

That is a rather startling sentiment, coming from a Christian minister, and I read rapidly on, finally heaving a sigh of relief when I discovered that, judging the matter from the statements of theatre-goers, from newspaper criticisms, from the bill-boards, and from conversation with one of the most distinguished of modern actors, Dr. Parkhurst, thus unprejudiced, has been led to conclude "that if the American theatre were suddenly to omit all its vicious accompaniments, and to come out frankly upon the ground of unequivocal purity, the theatre-going world would withdraw in impatient disgust, and the whole business would go into the hands of a receiver inside of a month"!

Now that, in a nutshell, is the whole case against the theatre. You may think what you please, young folks, about the ideal theatre. You may hold that when Sophocles wrote his "Antigone" and Æschylus his "Prometheus" and Euripides his "Medea," the drama was a powerful stimulus to lofty thought and noble action. You may exalt Shakespeare to the stars, and find all the force you please in King Lear, the most delightful poetry in the Midsummer Night's Dream, the deepest philosophy in Hamlet. That has absolutely nothing to do with the question of the modern theatre.

The opposition of Christians to the theatre is not an opposition to Shakespeare, but to "Camille"; not an opposition to Edwin Booth, but to —— with her almost annual divorces, and to —— with his drunkenness, and to —— with his lowest of intrigues. It is not opposition to an ideal, an impossible, theatre, but to the theatre as it is and as it is likely to continue.

And the more knowledge a pure-minded Christian gets of the present-day theatre, the less he will wish to have to do with it—as long, that is, as he remains a pure-minded Christian.

## CHAPTER XIV.

#### TIPSY-TOED RECREATION.

IN my list of false amusements I must give a prominent place to the dance. All dancing, like all Gaul, is divided into three parts. One-third is æsthetic, one-third is physical exercise, one-third is sensual. As to the first, the enjoyment of fine music, of beautiful dresses, forms, and motions, they may all be had under better auspices than in the dance. A woodland ramble, a tennis tournament, an archery club, bicycle or horseback riding, the concert-room,— these furnish in God's own way tenfold more beauty to the eye and ear than is furnished by the finest ball ever given. As for the second third, the physical exercise, it is ill timed, ill placed, ill environed. Hot air, gaslight, excitement, midnight, crowds, loaded supper tables, noise,—these make a poor outfit for a gymnasium.

Every honest investigator of the dance as now practised in America will agree that the third part into which this heathen Gaul is divided is the stronghold of the province. The sensuality of the dance makes bold-eyed women of soft-eyed maidens; it makes swaggering rakes of pure lads; it changes love to flirtation and a game of flippant shrewdness; it makes applicable to manly America Tolstoi's terrific strictures on ignoble Russia. It never re-creates a Christian; it dis-creates a Christian, and creates a sensualist.

Mr. Davidson, the evangelist, was once talking to a group of seminary girls about becoming Christians, and one objection they raised was that if they joined the church they would be obliged to give up dancing.

"No," he replied, "no one would object to you girls dancing together."

"O, but there's no fun in *that!*" honestly exclaimed one girl, without stopping to think.

The answer disclosed, in a way that girl was probably far from realizing, the tremendous peril of the dance. Men understand it well enough. They know how slight would be the attraction of the dance if conducted as in the wise old days of Greece, long lines of maidens alone, facing long lines of lads alone, out of doors in God's daylight. They know well enough that it is as easy to square the circle as to convert young people, that have begun to waltz, from the round dance to the square dance. And they understand perfectly in what ways and for what reasons the round dance is the round mouth of the pit.

It is not pleasant to dwell on this theme, nor is it likely to be profitable. A word—to the wise—is sufficient, while upon the unwise a Niagara of words would have no effect. If one is really bent upon being a pure-minded, pure-lived man or woman, a hint is enough to point out the danger, and clear eyes and unvitiated brain will speedily clinch the hint. If one has already become habituated to the ballroom, however, he has learned to estimate ability not by the head but by the foot, and he carries his conscience not in his breast but in his toes, where he dances upon it till he has pounded it to death.

While it is true that no girl would permit herself to be photographed in the act of waltzing with a young man, let her not allow such a photograph to find place in the gallery of the recording angel. Until a young man can find a dancer that will gladly walk as far to church as he will dance any night in a ballroom, let him, as he values his manhood and all his eternal interests, leave the ballroom and the dance peremptorily alone.

## CHAPTER XV.

### GAMES OF CHANCE.

I WAS once off camping with a merry party of business men, most of them in professional life, and the majority of them ministers. We spent our evenings in many ways, but the favorite amusement was dominoes. We discovered in ourselves a surprising fondness for that exceedingly mild form of amusement, and after each day's fishing, swimming, and mountain-climbing, we went back to our twos and sixes and nines with a zest that had come down to us unimpaired from the happy days of childhood.

Now dominoes, to my apprehension, is a game of chance. There were those in our party that hotly disputed the assertion, but they were the ones that always beat! If there is any element of skill in it, it is so reduced by the small number of pieces that fall to one by lot as to come very near the capacity of an idiot. It *is* a game of chance,—and the luck was against me!

Yet we all enjoyed it, and the game did us

good. We were brain-weary, and though some of us played chess, we had no business to. What we needed was something to occupy our minds without taxing them, something to serve as a nucleus for merry jests, to bring us all together around the one rickety table, and hold our eyes open until it was something like a decent time to go to bed.

But since we have come home, I will warrant that not one of us has touched a domino; no, not even Dr. Peace, who was most enthusiastic over "that nice, little, intellectual game." We have settled down to our preaching and editing and teaching and lawyering, and we are getting our brains into condition for dominoes and the Maine woods—next summer.

We might have played backgammon up there, and that would have been as much a game of chance as dominoes. We might have played portrait authors, and there would have been a strong element of chance in that, also. We might have played crokinole, and that would have rested our minds while wearying our fingers, and there would have been no chance in it.

*But we didn't play cards.*

And why? Not because cards would not have done for us just what dominoes did. Indeed, whist would have been a game far too intellectual for that company; we needed something more inane. But we left cards alone, even there in the Maine wilderness, because of what they stand for; because not a man of us could look at a pack of cards without thinking of ruined lives, of greasy saloon tables, of drawn pistols, of heart-broken mothers, of starving wives, of little children shrinking at the very name of the disgraced father; because with that pack of cards is indissolubly linked the fearful curse of gambling, and we did not wish to darken our pleasure with such memories, or befoul our rest with such associations.

There are games enough, thanks to the patent office and the keen, brisk brains behind it. I, for one, will not have the wailings of the lost shrieking through my hours of relaxation, nor, till memory and imagination leave me, can I fail to connect the thought of degradation, misery, and ruin, with the very sight of a pack of cards.

"That is bigoted," some of you are thinking peevishly. "Doesn't he know that some of the very best families play cards?" Of course I do, but if some of the best families play cards, so, also, do all of the worst families. "But people could gamble with anything, with chess," you urge. Well, when they begin to gamble with chess, I think it would be good policy for folks who wish to oppose gambling to refrain from chess. If meat makes my brother to offend, I will eat no meat. If that is bigoted, so is essential Christianity. Much that is not inherently wrong is made wrong by association with evil. For instance, I know of nothing essentially bad in a green screen back of a doorway, but a baker would be thought a queer business man who adopted that bit of saloon furniture. So I think a Christian, as a matter of business policy in the advertising of the Father's business, had better steer clear of everything that smells of the devil as distinctly as does a pack of cards.

I have another reason for my position. There is not in existence a game of cards that is worth playing by a man or woman who has any brains, or wit, or thoughtfulness, or anything in the upper story but rooms to let. "Why," you ask, "must there not be good mental drill in these card games?" No. "Why, how do you know?" you ask again. Because I have tried them, and found out their emptiness by experience. Now I hope you are not saying with the boy in the old Greek story, "I, too, want to find out their emptiness by experience," because I am not at all proud of the experience, but would give much if I could honestly say that I do not know a king from a jack, or poker from euchre. It will save you, young Christian, from many an embarrassment, if you are able to say that you know nothing of these devil's games.

Take my word for it,—born of a pretty thorough knowledge of every one of these games,—there is not as much fun or recreative value in the entire lot of them, the whole range from whist to high-low-jack, as there is in halma, or chess, or checkers, or logomachy, or any one of a score of games besides. They require little memory, less skill, no wit; they lead to that craven reliance upon luck which is a destruction of moral stamina; they cultivate one's powers of deception, of braggadocio and effrontery; and in the presence of the scores of noble indoor games, the use of these silly, senseless bits of pasteboard in any family is a severe commentary upon the thoughtfulness, vivacity, and brains of that household.

But cards are not the only game of chance. Nowadays people in fashionable and respectable society in this country no longer put down their pence or shillings or pounds around the whist or cribbage tables, as was perfectly proper not long ago. O, no! We have grown much better. We no longer play for stakes, we no longer "rake in pools"; we are more "progressive," you know, and we have "prizes."

"Progressive" euchre and halma and tennis and what not,—they are only progressive gambling.

Mr. Marion Lawrance, at an interesting convention, drew a good distinction between a prize and a reward. A reward, he said, all may get who attain a certain degree of excellence. A prize only one can get. God, in all His universe of blessings, has no single prize; but He has myriads of rewards, ready for all who will work hard enough for them. The essence of gambling lies not by any means in the element of chance; it lies in getting something for nothing, or in getting something that is not the appropriate and natural reward of the effort. The fitting reward of a game of tennis is an invigorated body and the pleasure and praise of skill. There is no connection of appropriateness or desert between a game of tennis and a pretty gold pin. If the hostess wishes to make presents, let her make them in such a way that they will go directly to the person that she likes. If she wishes to show off, let her do it in some other way than by opening a gambling establishment. If you play at all, play games whose interest and value need no increase from such false and dangerous sources. Have nothing to do with any game of chance.

## CHAPTER XVI.

#### PLAYING AT LOVE.

CANNOT name all false sports, but only typical ones, and stop with them; yet there is one more amusement, widely prevalent, about which I must say a word. Of all apologies for sport, the most mischievous is, I believe, flirting, playing at love. Do you not know that there are thousands of young men and women, and even—so contagious is any evil—even little boys and girls, in every part of our nation, whose sole amusement is this playing at love?

There is nothing good, you know, for which Satan's mint has not turned out some counterfeit. Flirting is the devil's counterfeit of love. It is the nearest that Satan ever comes to that sacred joy; but it is not the nearest that the flirter comes to Satan, for the mischief of flirtation is the mischief of a spark of fire, that grows.

Good love, like the good wine of the old proverb, needs no bush; that is, it needs no sign of its indwelling. You cannot hide it, any more than you can hide murder. But flirtation hangs out a sign in front of an empty inn, or worse, an inn filled with seven spirits of evil. If flirtation is your recreation, then you seek recreation, renewing, in what is essentially destructive; and as you sport with passion, and dally with light glances, and play with edged words that may mean very much or very little, you are gradually exiling yourself forever from all the love and happiness of honest-spoken men and loyal-hearted women.

For one of the meanest, most contemptible wretches on earth is the person who makes love with no intention of marrying. Play with fire, if you will. It won't hurt you so much as to play with a warm human heart. Fool with live wires, if you want to. It is not half so dangerous as to fool with the lightning flashes of admiring eyes and the electric touch of over-friendly hands. Waltz on the crumbling edge of Niagara, if you would like to. That is infinitely safer than dancing with heedless feet beside the whirling cataract of temptation.

Marriage is holy; courtship, therefore, should be as holy; *is* as holy, when it is genuine. But this miserable pretence of courtship is all unholy and devilish.

"But suppose the other party understands

the game? Suppose we are sure that he—or she—is no more in love than we are, and is simply flirting, as we are, for a little amusement?" I hear some one ask. To which question I have two replies to make:

1. You have no way of finding out whether the other party is in earnest or not. No one ever confessed to the person with whom he or she was making love that it was all a pretence. In fact, no one would flirt at all if the deception were not so close upon reality as to be hard to distinguish from it. Some of the greatest harm I have ever known to come from flirting has come from two flirters flirting together. You can never flirt—*with any one*—without running a risk of inspiring the passion you are imitating. And even if both of you are merely making believe, then,—

2. There are two fools, and two rogues, instead of one. God is love. Flirting is a graven image of God, a travesty on the most sacred thing in all the universe. You have no more right to pretend being in love than to pretend being honest, or good, or generous, when you are not. We all agree that an insincere Christian does more harm to Christianity than a hundred sincere infidels. So also an insincere lover does more harm to the great cause of love than a hundred sincere haters.

There is a language of friendship, and another quite different language of love. There is no excuse for confounding the two. Look brightly and merrily upon each other all you please, and sharply, too, with an eye to a possible future together; but there are looks that in God's eyes are criminal unless you have made up your mind to seek that united future. Let your hand-shakes be frank and hearty, no cold, kid-glove abominations; but there are hand-clasps that God's hand will avenge unless the heart goes with them. Talk to each other, young men and maidens, as long and earnestly as you will, and about the most serious matters; in no better way can you learn who will most happily join you in the great life dialogue; but there are words—yes, even light and jesting words—that if spoken by one who has no mind to speak the solemn words of the marriage service, are simply words of terrible guilt, recorded with tears on the great Book in heaven. Do not play at love-making.

With this I must close my catalogue of mischievous sports, though there are many other false amusements, if one only had time for the discussion. To some, dress is the sole amusement, and their one recreation a new necktie or cape or hat or ribbon. Others smoke to rest themselves, and thus play at weakening of muscles, shredding of nerves, and enfeeblement of brain. Still others sport with the impossible adventures of Dick Deadeye, the Detective, or the languid sentimentalities of Susy Silly, the Blue-eyed Beauty of Bellefontaine. Others get their enlivenment by leaning against the brick side of a store, watching people go by, and wondering what every one finds to do, or by infinitesimally minute discussions of everything around the grocery stove. There are false sports as numberless as fools and dandies and the shiftless.

A false sport is any amusement that may not be just as amusing for all as for one. A false sport is any amusement that develops bad habits or qualities, or fails to develop good ones. Let us learn to choose those recreations that create.

## CHAPTER XVII.

#### FUN ALIVE AND FUN DEAD.

IT was on a beach in New Jersey. A party of young people were romping in the surf. They whispered together, "Let's duck her!" No sooner planned than done. Down went the luckless girl, held by the mischievous jokers, who rushed back, screaming with laughter, to the beach. They waited, looking out over the surf, in expectation that a dripping, scolding girl would rise and follow them in; but the girl never rose, nor had they, at the time when the newspapers printed the story, found her body.

That is a case of what would have been called, but for the "accident," "fun alive." It turned out to be fun dead. What is the difference? and how can we be sure that our "fun alive" will never become fun dead? Let me tell you.

Fun alive, like a living person, is just as fine to look upon to-morrow as to-day. Fun dead decays faster than a corpse.

Fun alive talks and laughs boldly. Fun dead is as secret as a ghost's gliding movements.

Fun alive has a heart that beats warmly for the other fellow. Fun dead has no pulse.

Fun alive has brains that are in good working order. Fun dead has no brains at all; they have been removed by the undertaker.

Fun alive has eyes that can see into the future. Fun dead is blind as any skull in the graveyard,—blind to all consequences and to all possibilities.

Fun alive has nerves,—nerves of sympathy, nerves of tact, nerves of love. Fun dead prides himself on not being nervous.

Fun alive has a smile; fun dead has a grin.

Fun alive says, "What sport for him!" Fun dead says, "What a grind on him!"

Fun alive makes friends; fun dead makes foes.

And finally, fun alive enlivens his master, while fun dead makes his master, every day more and more, just such a malicious, ugly skeleton as himself.

## CHAPTER XVIII.

#### FUN AFOOT.

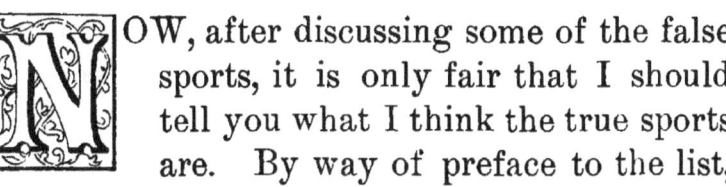OW, after discussing some of the false sports, it is only fair that I should tell you what I think the true sports are. By way of preface to the list, let me make the obvious suggestion that for a man or woman of sedentary work, out-of-door sports should predominate, while those whose work brings into play the muscles and the lungs may rest satisfied with a larger proportion of mental games. Yet it is not true that an author, for example, should do no reading for recreation, only that his physical sports should be in excess of his mental play; nor that a carpenter should not enjoy his game of baseball, for example, only that he would be wise to take the greater part of his play with a book.

As I cannot discuss all sports, since there are so many, I shall be egotistical of necessity, and shall speak of the sports that I know best, because they form my own recreation. They will serve just as well for examples. And first, for outdoor amusements.

At the head of my list of sports stands no game at all, only walking.

I bless God daily for a pair of feet cornless, bunionless, willing and strong; for a good shoemaker; for a pair of boots that covers the whole earth with leather; and for God's wide, wonderful world to which these blessings give me pleasant access. In walking I have an amusement which costs nothing but sole leather; which is dependent on no tools, mechanism, or implements; which can be carried on in all weathers, all seasons, all times of day, with company or without, for a long time or short, slowly or rapidly, carelessly or thoughtfully; which fits my days of health or of sickness, of joy or gloom; an amusement that may be made to minister to a love for science, which may fill my geological cabinet or my insect cases, and my head as well; a recreation that puts me in most serene and delightful converse with kindly nature in all her witching changes; that cleanses and expands the cramped lungs, sends the gay blood bounding to the farthest capillary, hardens the muscles, and disciplines the will.

What a loss people permit themselves when they permit themselves the loss of their feet! I am sometimes half inclined to the opinion of Ruskin, who cursed all inventions, bicycle, railroad, electric engine, cable cars and what not, designed to supplant human feet on the earth God gave us to tread. Ruskin was not venting a cynical snarl at our modern civilization, but merely at that undoubted tendency of it to allow machinery to weaken men and enfeeble women.

To be sure, the steam horse can rattle me in an hour a distance over which shank's horses could scarcely transport me in six hours; but it lands me less of a man than when I started, with quivering nerves, aching head, dust-filled eyes, disordered digestion, and thorny temper. Shank's horses land me more of a man than when I started, with clearer brain, more cheerful, exultant temper, stronger body, a firmer grasp on life, a keener sense of this beautiful world, and a closer knowledge of God. That is what Ruskin means,—that machinery is dear at the cost of manhood.

What pleasures, too, are open to the walker, which the foot-tied must resign! He may see the sunset from the highest hilltops; he is the first to note the spring flowers, the changes wrought by the winter floods. He can watch the rarest birds in their shyest haunts.

If to his walking your pedestrian add the ability to trot smartly for a mile or two, he is well equipped indeed. If walking has not sent oxygen to the most distant nook of his lungs, running will. If walking has not drawn tense his muscles, running will. There are just two faults to find with it; for it might as well be acknowledged that there is no perfect sport, outdoors or in. One cannot talk much while one is running, nor indulge to any great extent in the contemplation of nature. Let it be acknowledged, too, that both walking and running, though they might well make a giant of a pigmy as to the matter of legs and feet, would leave him a pigmy still in regard to arms.

So the well-furnished player must have other sports at his disposal, not only to remedy these defects, but also for variety, which is the cinnamon and cloves and nutmeg of life. For just as one should have a vocation, to be sure, but also an avocation, so one should have not merely a recreation, but an ab-recreation, a side recreation, to which he can turn when the chief sport goes awry. My ab-recreations are two, the bicycle and tennis, and each deserves a chapter.

## CHAPTER XIX.

RECREATION ON TWO WHEELS.

THE bicycle was hailed on its advent as furnishing the ideal exercise, equally, and without undue stress, developing all parts of the body; while at the same time, by its delightful motion through swiftly varying scenes, it furnished a constant fascination to the mind. But for the naturalist, who wishes to note the precise marking on the wing of that butterfly which just alighted on the thistle yonder, who wants to pick up every slab of fossiliferous limestone to scan it for rare denizens, who is perpetually on the lookout for flowers, grasses, leaves, not yet in his herbarium,—for all such queer gentry the bicycle is a little too swift.

Furthermore, when two friends would like to converse, bicycles make very unsympathetic listeners. I have tried many topics of conversation while on the wheel, and the only topic that seems to agree with the fancy of that tricksy creature is herself. Talk of cranks and pedals, bearings, gearings, tire, spoke, Columbia, and Victor, and the egotistic machine is all right and listens purring. Begin to discuss a book, the landscape, the latest scandals, and she runs into ruts, and develops portentous squeaks, and tries to climb over every stone in the road.

Yet further; to one who would be easy master of his sport, that it may attend him when and where he choose, the bicycle is a cumbrous servant. He must woo it ever with oil and monkey-wrench and cleaning cloth and spoke-tightener, watch rain and rust, make friends with the man who does repairing, that the bill may not bankrupt him; and with all his care, a lost nut, or a broken ball, or a bent pin, or a little rain or snow or dust may balk him of his fun.

But still, when all this is said, about the most imperial sensation mortal man may attain is felt by a good rider on a good wheel over a good road. All muscles are at pleasurable tension, the breeze whistles through his hat, the fence-posts sway in excitement as he flashes by, the trees wave their congratulations, and it seems the comical hope of Darius Green come true, the realization of the old Dædalian myth; and one has but to fear that, like the impetuous Icarus, he may fly too near the sun, and melt off his rubber tire.

I can imagine no finer summer outing than a small party of wheelmen can contrive, with light suit, light baggage, light heart, a leap into the saddle, and off for the Smoky Mountains, for Canada, for the Mammoth Cave,— for any place you please to which roads lead. Halt where nightfall catches you, in queer country inn or farmhouse, and off in the morning early, with delightful uncertainty as to what will next turn up, lofty hill, blossoming meadows, cool ravine, or smoking factories; on through the long, bright day, past hurrahing boys, busy farms, housewives glancing up from the ironing-table; through fresh morning into wide-eyed noon and the sacred evening, and then to soundest and most refreshing slumber. A summer outing with the bicycle is one of the best care-dispellers and cheer-compellers man's brain ever invented. And the essence of such a tour, the spirit that made the Pickwick Papers famous, reposes forever in the pneumatic tire, though it never make a century run. The magic steed has rendered the neighboring city as accessible as the grocery store used to be, and has brought the entire county into your front yard. The bliss of the bird is yours, in such measure as only the coming flying machine will surpass. Before breakfast, if you are enterprising, you will take a flight, and your brain will "babble o' green fields" in a happy undertone all day. And when your labor is over you will take another flight, and the panorama of Sunset Hill or the music of Willow Brook will enrich and soothe your slumber. Two vacation outings every day—that is the blessed privilege of every owner of a bicycle.

## CHAPTER XX.

#### OUT IN THE OPEN.

MY other ab-recreation, side-recreation, is lawn tennis. For this, also, as well as the bicycle, perfection has been claimed, in that it exercises equally and moderately all portions of the body. But, as I have said, there is no perfect game. Conversation, which is a possible joy of walking, is banished from lawn tennis, as from the bicycle; for you can hardly call conversation such beggarly elements as "Serve," "Ready," "You receive," "Out," and "Thirty all." Nor does tennis unroll before you a fair panorama of ever-varying scenes; it is a stationary game. Nor is tennis, either, a recreation independent of circumstances. You must have a friend, or, better, three of them. Lines must be maintained against the rain, court be rolled or cut, nets repaired, a racket kept well strung; and lawn tennis, like cycling, is at the mercy of the clouds.

Yet, season and circumstances favoring, the game deserves its origin; it is a royal sport.

It maintains one's interest unflagging, it calls for ever-increasing skill, it has possibilities of infinite variety and surprises, it finds place for the greatest strength and agility, and can be played with equal zest by the weak and clumsy. It is a social and jovial game. It develops gracefulness and pleasing courtesy, and is a valuable accession to the equipment of any man or woman.

Those are my own favorite outdoor sports: walking, running, cycling, and tennis. But in naming these as samples of what I mean by a rational physical amusement, I exhaust the list precisely as little as I would exhaust the list of eatables by naming my favorite dishes. There are scores of valuable recreations I have not even tasted, and those I have suggested, though probably the most useful and adaptable of all, might for many persons be far from the best.

There is our national game, which, though the nation need not be exceedingly proud of it, is a good and healthy sport, if *you* play it and do not merely look on, and if you *play* it and do not change it into a profession. There is football, manly and vigorous, a matchless school for the temper, and an incomparable drill in disciplined activity. There is the little known lacrosse, less rude and violent, but requiring more skill and dexterous strength than either. There are cricket and boating; there are archery, and fishing, and skating, and bowling, and riding on horseback; and there are innumerable lesser sports, like throwing of quoits, old-time croquet, the mild-mannered bean-bag, and the countless school games, hare and hounds, wolf, and so on, *ad infinitum*. I have a catholic mind for all of these. I enjoy watching them zealously played, and so will any lover of hearty humanity. Choose out from the host of them two or three, and devote yourself to these, that your skill may become a pleasure and an assurance of zest and pride. Having chosen these two or three, suited to your age, employment, tastes, and fancied dignity, put yourself on the best of terms with them, and use them through all your busy life as ministers of health and vigor and good cheer.

## CHAPTER XXI.

#### ESTABLISHING OUR MACKINACS.

T is fitting to close this series of chapters on fun outdoors with a word or two about vacations,—the right kind and the wrong kind.

You cannot see your way to getting a vacation, dear Howard Hardwork and Dorothy Drudge? Then surely you need a word of consolation, if I can find one for you, and I think I can. For, do you know? in not taking a vacation you are far nearer the primitive order of things, the good old ways, than we favored folk that can take one. Read your Ten Commandments. Does not the fourth commandment provide as clearly for six days of work in the week as for one day of rest? This great vacation of one day in seven, of fifty-two whole days in the year, we too little appreciate, I fear. Indeed, most of us hardly look upon them as a vacation at all, but long after some two weeks or two months that we can have somewhere in a lump, unspoiled by any work.

Ah, God's way is best; God's way, that fits to each rest its toil, to each toil its rest. We are in sore need of vacations in modern times, beloved, because we do not work in the right way, in God's way. Goethe's famous phrase, "unhasting, unresting," gives a hint of what that way is. Christ's phrases, "My Father worketh hitherto and I work," and "It is My meat and drink to do the will of My Father," give still clearer hints of the right way to work. Christ got His meat and drink, His joy, His vacation, by way of His work; and so may we.

But when we overwork, this cannot be done. Neither can it when we overplay, nor when we worry or fret, or are filled with envy or tormented with ambition, or affrighted with doubts. How often we say from our hearts, "It is not work that kills, but worry." It is not work that cries for vacations, but worry.

If you can manage to work as God would have you work, my dear Howard Hardwork and Dorothy Drudge,—if you can manage to trust God for the strength of the day and the fortune of the morrow, to be cheery and smiling and prayerful and loving,—then I will risk you with no vacation whatever, but one day in seven. And, more than that, if God does not see best to give you any longer vacation, I do not believe you will even think of wanting it.

But for most of us vacations are possible, if not every year, then in the delightful "once in a while"; and surely in this book some word should be said about the right use of them.

I spent a week one summer on the island of Mackinac. Maybe you don't know where that fairy island is. Look on your maps at the junction of the three greatest of the Great Lakes,—Michigan, Huron, and Superior. Just where the breezes from all three can sweep over it with their full cargo of health and freshness is a little dot that resolves itself, as the steamer approaches it, into one of the most beautiful islands in the world.

It is a rocky bit, "ringed about by sapphire seas," with delightful glimpses, everywhere through the birches and evergreens, of the sparkling water. Historic charms are here added to the charms of nature,—the old trading-station, the battle-grounds where English and Americans had it out, the houses where dwelt the heroines of Marion Harland and Constance Fenimore Woolson.

You can see that I enjoyed myself there by the way I run on about it. But what I want to say is this:

## ESTABLISHING OUR MACKINACS. 93

When I got back to Boston, I found that my vacation had only begun. Mackinac kept repeating itself. In the midst of all the heat of the sweltering city during the dog-days I constantly was receiving breezes from that invigorating island. It was much to know that *somewhere* there was coolness. While walking through the narrow streets, often noisome with bad odors, it was much to know that somewhere was fragrance,—balmy arbor vitæ, and flowers distilling honey in the sunshine. While fretted with many cares, the mere thought of the peace and quiet over yonder on that enchanted island was enough to soothe my spirit and refresh my body. And so, you see, my vacation is being prolonged, and I guess it will last forever.

Now all our pleasant experiences ought to be very much like this, and they may be made so by the shrewd use of memory. I could not stay forever at Mackinac; but in that delightful week I had established my spiritual Mackinac, and, firmly as that lovely island is rooted in the Great Lakes, I had fixed in my life this immaterial Mackinac, which is the most real one after all. I go to it often enough to know that it is there, and to ensure the prolongation of it through all my living.

And O, this is a great thing in the midst of

all the busy, fretting, anxious hours of this life, to know that there is a resting-place awaiting us, that peace is there, and good cheer, and fragrance, and song, and health, and newness of energy and courage. We have found them there often before; we may find them there again; and the memory and the anticipation prolong them through the periods when we are away from our Mackinacs. And there is no one so busy and no one so poor that he cannot build for himself a cottage on some island of happy memories.

## CHAPTER XXII.

#### HOW TO SPOIL A VACATION.

SPOILING vacations is a wonderfully popular amusement. It has always seemed to me a pity that folks should go about this matter in such an unmethodical, haphazard way. Everything, in this century, ought to be done in a scientific manner.

I fear I shall appear to be boasting, but I can assure you that a long, varied, and entirely successful course of experiment in vacation-spoiling entitles me to give directions on this subject worthy your implicit confidence. I know just how to do it.

In the first place, you must persuade yourself that vacations are made simply for you,— for your own tasks or amusements. But this qualification is already possessed by so many that it is hardly worth mentioning.

If you own that most efficient notion, you may safely dispense, in this task of vacation-spoiling, with perseverance and industry. When a man with a well-developed bump of selfishness sets out to spoil his vacation, it is wonderful how readily everything and everybody assist him. It's easier than rolling down hill.

I hope that before your vacation began you made very extensive plans for vacation work and play,—so extensive that they could not possibly be carried out, even with all men's acquiescence and aid. The failure of these ambitious designs through your own laziness, and the lack of co-operation on the part of the cruel world, will materially aid in spoiling your vacation.

Then it is absolutely necessary, in vacation, to lie long in bed, to rest. Keep this up conscientiously, especially through the hottest days. The freshness of the early morning is likely to spoil one's vacation-spoiling in spite of one's self.

Decide at the outset that fair skies and cool weather are essential to your happiness. You will thus enlist in your business of vacation-spoiling the winds, rains, clouds, and, in fact, all the forces of the solar system.

Eat and drink what you fancy, and much of it. Unless you are very unfortunate, that will save you all further trouble in the matter.

If, however, the vacation perversely remains unspoiled, do nothing about it. Indeed, do nothing at all. If, in hot weather, you read, or study, or sew, or make garden, you will run serious risk of failing to spoil your vacation. Take warning.

Of course, what is true regarding helping yourself is doubly true of helping other people. I have seen vacations, which were being spoiled in a very perfect and workmanlike manner, suddenly and disastrously renovated by an imprudent act of kindness. To be sure, those who do such things are beginners in the art; but be on your guard.

Stay indoors. There is something about green leaves and flowers and butterflies, insignificant though they seem, that is able to enliven and cheer even a skilled vacation-spoiler.

Above all, take no exercise, either by work or by play, especially in hot weather. If you did, your food might be well digested, and the energy of your nerves and muscles might be turned aside from those restless, mysterious twitchings which constitute one of the vacation-spoiler's most efficient allies.

The chief danger is that you may become interested in something, and then good-bye to all hope of spoiling your vacation. Maintain with your utmost indifference a state of complete apathy.

I will guarantee that the conscientious following of these simple instructions will never fail to result in a vacation gloriously and systematically spoiled.

## CHAPTER XXIII.

#### THE PLEASURES OF THE TONGUE.

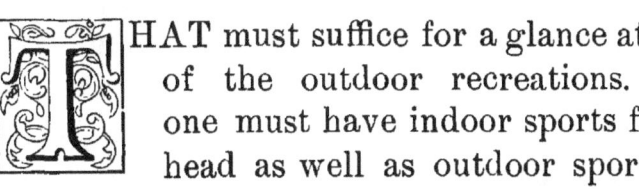HAT must suffice for a glance at some of the outdoor recreations. But one must have indoor sports for the head as well as outdoor sports for the body, and to these we must now turn. I will name first, as the chief in my theory, what is far from the chief in my practice,— conversation.

The supreme mental delight of a thoughtful man or woman should be conversation; but conversation, you know, is one of the lost arts. Need it be? Thinking is not by any means one of the lost arts, nor is writing of books or of letters, nor is the reading of both. But bring two thoughtful, reading people together, face to face, with absolutely nothing in the room, with curtains drawn to shut out exterior suggestions, and probably they will both sit there appalled by the conversational vacuity.

Can you imagine Columbus sitting down with one of his officers in their dark cabin after land had been sighted and a new world won,—sitting down, they two, with folded hands and mute or stammering tongues, at a loss for something to say? Can you fancy Stanley with his staff in mid-Africa grouped about the camp-fire in silence, embarrassed by lack of topics for conversation? We are living in a time when whole continents, entire worlds, of thought and enterprise, of achievement and anticipation, are spread out in clear light or in provoking half-revelation before every wide-awake mind. There is not a man or a woman with healthy brain who may not have wonders of discovery matching those of Columbus or Stanley. And that we should sit about our camp-fires, embarrassed for lack of something to talk about! That we should not meet as friends in a company of goldhunters, to gloat over each rich find, each discovered treasure!

Our papers and magazines are crowded with announcements of inventions and scientific discoveries, and not alone in the realm of the physical is there wizardry at work. Every magazine you take up flashes to the seeing eye with glints of a great social and spiritual fire kindled anew in these modern days with sparks carried over from that first great century, fire of love to God and love to man, renovating our social order, making war on warfare, trying judicial systems in higher scales than theirs, remodeling governments, evangelizing the globe. We read carelessly the burning pages whose every line, five centuries ago, would have caused an intellectual earthquake, lay our fat finger on the page and pass it to our neighbor with a yawn. "Have you read that? That's the latest." Triumph of modern conversation!

For this keenest of all intellectual recreation but three things are necessary, all to be bought without money, yet with price,—a mind wide-awake, a friend like-minded, and an unselfish, unegotistic sympathy between you two. If you can gain those three things, you need never lack inspiring mental renewing.

But they are not easy to gain, and therefore it is that conversation is becoming a lost art. To converse well, and take pleasure in talking, one must know something thoroughly,—not a mere surface knowledge, good for no more than three sentences and an adjective; not a knowledge of books by titles and reviews, or of events by newspaper head lines, or of discoveries by stray paragraphs, but a knowledge that has its roots in genuine interest, its trunk solidified by persistent study, its leaves expanded in the free air of eager, original thinking. Smatter-brained folks cannot converse well.

The chief requirement for conversation, however, is sympathy. Unless you are willing to be interested in your friend's interests and he in yours, unless you have imagination enough to put yourself in his place and he in yours, unless you can give up your fads and hobbies, your private worries and individual ecstasies, and he his, you two may interchange monologues by the hour but you cannot get together, you cannot converse. But if you two are able, with the frank, spontaneous joy of childhood, to roam hand in hand through the forest of universal thought, plucking here and there a flower and often looking up to the sky, if you really can put your minds together for delight in mutual treasures, for intellectual fellowship and spiritual inspiration, then, ah, then, you will have won for yourselves one of the purest pleasures, one of the noblest recreations, this life can furnish a weary body or an exhausted brain.

## CHAPTER XXIV.

#### READING THAT RECREATES.

"QUITE a lot of murders, eh, yesterday?" It was a man in the car who glanced up from his newspaper to address the casual remark to his comrade; and that comrade took his eyes away from his own blanket sheet long enough to grunt a careless assent.

"Quite a lot of murders!" mused the listener, as the train sped on. "What a fearful thing that is to say so glibly! The awful, growing madness; the horror of passions, hidden yet gnawing; the dark broodings, the lightning flash of the deed, the sudden terror of flight; the utter misery of homes, the agony of sorrow and shame, the stern courtroom and cold cell, the plunge into a black future,—'Quite a lot of murders, eh, yesterday?'"

Are the newspapers hardening people's hearts? Is it good for us that telegraph wires should groan over land and under sea with such sad burdens of human crime only that we may glance lightly at the shocking record?

These things are startling. They readily catch the reporter's eye and the public pennies. They present their claim as news with an assurance that seems irresistible. Good deeds hide modestly in corners, and only the wise and skilful can unearth them; but any bungler of the pen and jerker of the telegraph key can give a murder currency.

What does it mean to give murders currency, to make them run? It means just what it would mean if excursions were organized to scenes of murders, and the whole world set down to hobnob with the murderer. Only, it is easier to make the murder run about the world, than to get the world to run to the murder. With modern arts of picture and of pen one way is just as vivid as the other.

The newspapers claim that the photographic methods of the press really tend to discourage crime and make it abhorrent. "Why should not a faithful picture of a horrible deed horrify men?" they ask. They forget the influence of familiarity. If the newspapers should agree among themselves to report but one murder a year, the fearful exhibition might fill men with horror; but when murders are part of our daily reading, it comes to "Quite a lot of murders, eh, yesterday?"

If a young man or a young woman cares

anything for the possession of emotions rightly delicate and fitly sensitive, he will not permit the newspapers to put him in the position of a police judge or of the inspecting officer of a prison. If the natural shrinking from sin is a feeling to be preserved, many a newspaper must be shunned as a plague. This is not saying that we must withhold ourselves from contact with sinners when we have opportunity of helping them. Newspaper accounts of crime are not read with such motives, and do not inspire such desires.

Let every young Christian exercise great care in the selection of his newspaper. No papers are free from fault in this direction, but some are much worse than others. Let him, quite regardless of politics or secular interests, read only those papers that reduce their mention of crime to a minimum; and many young men and women of quick imagination and ready emotion would do a wise thing if they got their news entirely from the admirable summaries of the great, clean weeklies.

In fine, as there is a reading that recreates, certainly there is also a reading that discreates, and the average newspaper furnishes that reading in abundance. Therefore I assuredly would not read newspapers for sport.

But you do not, you declare; you read them for study and for information. Study of what? Those long rows of men, tipped back against the wall in the offices of all hotels, those hundreds who daily pass through your town on the cars, their weary eyes glued to the papers held in their shaking hands, those crowds in the drug-stores, the markets, the cobblers' shops, on the street corners, gathered about the fortunate possessors of the wondrous sheet,—upon what are all these mature minds feeding? What information are they seeking? What science are they studying?

For an answer do not go to the men, do not note their respectability or their virtue or their intelligence, do not ask them their purposes, because all these matters are not to the point; but go to the paper itself, and analyze the columns of any daily that you please in this fair land, this Christian land; and by the statistics of the yardstick, if by nothing higher, by the topics discussed on these mystic leaves, and by the proportionate space given them, judge what science these men are studying so absorbingly. It is the science of murder, or of horrible executions therefor. It is the science of the ward politician and his various tricks. It is the science of unsavory tales of scandal, of social impurity, of wrecked lives.

It is the science of theft, embezzlement, burglary; the science of accident, of crushed limbs and mangled bodies; the science of tornado, of fire, of earthquake; the science of assassination, of war and rumors of war; the science of Bill Bruiser and of bloody noses; of horse-flesh debasing human flesh; of quarrels and gambling and liquor dens; of unfounded political rumors; of stocks and deals and combines and gambling, most infernal because most cruel and disastrous; the science of criminality and horror and small talk. That is what they are studying. Nor are they studying all this with any purpose to make it better, which would be some palliation. The newspaper does not teach scorn of Bill Bruiser; does not devote itself to the suppression of stock-gambling; does not spend its energies in inquiring how Johnny Malone, whose criminal deed it gloates over, may be made a better boy; in short, in chronicling so persistently the vicious and depraved and deplorable side of human existence, it is not engaged with all its heart, nor with a fraction of its heart, in bettering the evil. In the meantime, these men are not studying the science of good government, the needs of our brothers and sisters down in the filth, the gospel of our Lord and the coming of His kingdom. Away with the flimsy pretence that this enormous amount of newspaper-reading is done in pursuit of information or of knowledge. It is for amusement, amusement low, vicious, sensual.

There is but one rational way in which to read a newspaper, and that, as Dr. Clark suggests, is after the fashion of reading bills in Congress, which are often read by title only. Reading a newspaper by title takes a Christian never more than fifteen minutes. The mere headings of most of the columns should be to him great danger signs. No. Let us be honest if to us, as to so many millions, newspaper-reading is an amusement; and let us own up that we do it because we like it. Is it not a cruel sport to get our pleasure out of the woe and wickedness of the world, out of its sneers and petty scandals, out of its horrors and follies? In advising you how to play, can I do otherwise than warn you away from such devil's play as this?

Now in spite of the fact that one is true (or supposed to be) and the other acknowledged to be false, everything I have said in warning against reading newspapers for sport applies to the indiscriminate reading of fiction. Novels, the whipped cream of literature, have become our mental bread and meat. We must have our history dressed up in the historical romance, our very sermons and philosophy must be disguised in the "story with a purpose." The effect upon our minds is the same as the effect of too much mince pie upon the small boy's stomach. For reading, to be permanently recreative, must be reading with a purpose,—reading with a purpose above recreation.

Who gets more enjoyment out of eating, the pampered millionaire, whose tongue is the wearied host for myriads of sugary, creamy, spicy guests, or the little daughter of the laborer, trotting about all the morning with helpful steps, who has come a long two miles with her father's dinner to eat it with him from a tin pail? And who gets the more pleasure out of reading, the satiated fiction-glutton, her brain crammed with disordered fragments of countless scenes of adventure, love, and tragedy, impatient of the same old situations, the familiar characters, the stale plots,—she, or the girl who is fired with a love for history, say, who wants to know all about the grand old, queer old Socrates, and then about his friends, and then about the times in which he lived, and then about the way in which they all lived, and then about the Socratic legacy to the ages? Why, will that girl ever be done with the feast? Can you not see, looking down on her joy with a blessing, the very Lord of the banquet, who has ordered all history and ordained that the truth He fashions shall be stranger always than the fictions man contrives?

Take the word of a man who has made full trial of both. Solid reading is as much more interesting and attractive than frivolous reading as solid living is more recreative than frivolous living. A full mind is never bored. It is only the frothy brain, honey-combed with fiction, tunneled mischievously with hollow unrealities, that is really bored. The great books of science,—what poetry is so poetic, what romance so romantic as these to the mind unvitiated by artificial tastes? To enter into the treasuries of the snow, the armories of the clouds, to gain admission to the council chambers of the elements, on the magic carpet of astronomy to travel to distant stars and more distant æons, to know the earth in its morning days, and see the flower hidden in the seed!

Or, if your reading must have more human interest, did ever hero of a novel live so wild a romance as Napoleon's? Was Henry Esmond or Colonel Newcome so lovable as Thackeray himself? Have Miss Alcott, Miss Larcom, Mrs. Stowe, written anything as entertaining as their own biographies? Was ever a story of adventure so marvelous as the real experience of Stanley? In all fiction is there a heroine to compare with Joan of Arc?

Why, when I would rest from joys of the mind too intense, when I become even satiated with mental exhilaration and want mental commonplace, I flee from the fairy-land of the real to the sober country of fiction, and find in the dull imaginings of Scott or Dickens or Thackeray or Shakespeare or Milton a relief from the too brilliant thoughts of the Creator, only swiftly to return again from their weak platitudes to the exuberant marvels of God's creation.

Thus reading—reading methodical and serious and solid—I earnestly recommend as an unparalleled mental recreation. A few pennies nowadays will buy the books, or, in these times of free libraries, they may be had for the taking, simply and cheaply, as all great gifts should be. What to read and how to read wisely—it would be a joy to write an entire book on the theme, a joy I propose to myself in continuance of this "How" series of books, if the public is sagacious enough to favor them; but it is far too large a subject to attack at the fag end of a chapter.

## CHAPTER XXV.

#### WRITING FOR FUN.

MY third mental recreation should be writing. Do you know that you do not know yourself until you push yourself outside of yourself and look at yourself? That is one thing for which conversation is useful; it enables you to get a fair impression of your mind, with all its brilliancy and dulness, its hastiness and pains-taking, its flaws and its beauties. "As a small boy empties his pockets to see what is in them," says Dr. Holmes, "so I talk to see what is in my mind." But writing sets out your very self before you in permanent, unmistakable black and white. If your spirit stammers, stutters, is inaccurate, stupid, dull, so splutters your pen, and such dull lines stare up at you from the telltale paper.

Moreover, writing does more than disclose the writer: it enlarges him. A life is doubled that is well written out in one's private journal. Its joys are greater, its pangs are softened. A life is quadrupled that is repeated in cordial, gay letters to one's friends. And if one's life has attained the magic multiplying mirror of the printing-press, who can tell how many times it is magnified to the good of the world?

Nowadays—as the editors tell us when they send back our manuscripts—nowadays every one is writing. And that is well, even if literally true, because every one also is reading, and every one is getting to think. Those are the three R's, you know: reading, the receptive; 'rithmetic, the thoughtful; and 'riting, the expressive,—the three R's, the three recreations, that is.

Do you know what joys are the most permanent in this world, the blessings handed down through the ages as most precious heirlooms, when paintings and temples and jewels and thrones are resigned to dust? They are bits of recorded human life, fragments of human joys and sorrows embalmed in biographies, histories, poems, and stories, in journals and letters. What is the great joy of the world may be the great joy of the individual. Not that we should all turn authors in the technical sense of the term, but that we should all come to know what the fortunate few have hitherto understood, the delight of expression.

Poetry? Yes, even poetry. The rhymsters of my acquaintance get a vast amount of enjoyment from their "home-roams" and their "given-rivens." The editors may send them all back with that cruel printed slip, but never mind. "'Tis better to have rhymed and been rejected, than never to have rhymed at all," as Tennyson might have said.

That, then, is my list of mental amusements,—conversing, reading, writing. I do not despise more labored indoor sports. I have a catholic taste for all of them, from music, checkers, chess, dominoes, crambo, logomachy, proverbs, portrait authors, spello, halma, to that sensible game with the very silly name, "tiddledy-winks." None are perfect; some are good for large groups, some for small, some for thoughtful people and some for the jovial, some for dexterity and some for wit, and some for ready knowledge. Lay up in your minds and houses a good supply of them, for they are rich treasures. Learn every one of them that is described in this book, and keep your eyes and ears open for more.

I have a mind to close this series of chapters with a six-sentence sermon. Why should there not be a wee mite of seriousness, even in this treatise on amusement? Listen, my brethren:

Recreation for mind and body is a part of God's plan for our living, made necessary by constant waste of mind and body, which require constant renewal. Do not expect to have health and cheer for nothing; they are bought with a price, as are all best things. You must pay time for them, and thoughtful planning, and eager energy. But when you have won the art of playing, then, let me urge you, go on to the higher art, the art that is born of this,—the art of putting your play into your work. Vigorous body and active mind, sparkling eye and kindly jollity, brain and body thus re-created daily,—this, the end of sport, is worthily so only as it is the beginning of manly and womanly toil. Only as our muscles, renewed by exercise, are strengthened for the wielding of God's tools, only as our quickened brains are enlivened for God's thinking, only as our buoyed spirits are exalted for Christlike, helpful living, has recreation won its crown of entire success.

## CHAPTER XXVI.

#### THE FAMILY ROUND TABLE.

PITY the family that does not possess some big, round table, about which to gather in the evening. This is a family altar of cheer that will do much to take the place of the old-fashioned roaring fireplace.

No so-called "centre-table" will answer, however beautiful and costly it may be. A marble-top table is an abomination for this purpose, good only for corners and bric-à-brac, absolutely worthless for school books and mother's work and the boys' games.

The family round table would best be the dining-table, if the dining-room is on the living floor, the table being adorned with a soft cover of some warm color. If the family round table is stationed here, there is no danger of interruption of the evening's arrangements for work and pleasure by chance callers that may come to see only one member of the family.

For the family round table there should be a good light,—one high enough above the table to send its rays over a generous circumference. There should be the soft cloth already mentioned, and, above all, the table should always be kept clear for action. If it is the dining-table, that will be the case. If it is a table in the sitting-room, it should not be made a permanent depository for books, magazines, and papers, work-basket, and household paraphernalia.

In a home thus furnished (and it is astonishing to see how many homes are lacking this particular) the game of tiddledy-winks is always in order; the desire for dominoes in not thwarted by lack of space; there is a place for John to work on his scrap-book, and for Jennie to work at her new quilt; there is a place for father to spread his newspaper, and for mother to lay her *Harper's;* there is an arena for jackstraws, and a round suggestive of crambo.

This family table gathers the household group, and binds them together in a magnetic circle of love and pleasure. There is something in the fact of its being a *round* table that no square table or oblong table can ever accomplish. If in order to get this family centre you must knock out all the bric-à-brac, and destroy the good looks of parlor or sitting-room, and even send to the attic the most expensive inlaid-top table, it would prove no loss, but a rich and permanent gain.

In these round-table games let the entire family join. If the high-pressure public schools mortgage the children's evenings, secure at any rate a half hour before bedtime, though they must graduate a whole year later. Father should have no business paper more urgent than this, and mother no mending so imperative. And if a neighbor happens in or is invited in, all the better.

There must be mutual giving up "around the evening lamp," a willingness to play others' favorite games though they are our pet aversions. Brains must be put into it all, and hearty good cheer. Have a tournament now and then, a whole series of games evening after evening, to create a serial interest. Keep a record of these games, a round-table chronicle, wherein conspicuous victories may be recorded, and wherein you may see what you were playing this time last year. That is, go into it with all your heart, and make it a strong feature of your home life.

How the children will look back upon it in coming years! What a university it will prove for them, quickening their minds at the same time that it warms their hearts! From your family round-table what knights and ladies may go forth, chivalrously to bear themselves in the battle of life!

## CHAPTER XXVII.

### THE HOME ORCHESTRA.

F I ever have to "board out," I mean to hunt up a musical family! They will be sweet-tempered there. And unselfish. And jolly.

I don't mean a family where one member—usually the grown-up daughter—does up the music for the entire household, strumming on the piano of an evening, to the destruction of all conversation and the confusion of the whole family life, while mamma looks up proudly from her sewing, and papa's nerves, racked by his day in the office, jump and twitch almost beyond endurance, and little Jack begs in vain for "just one game of carroms."

No, not that; I mean a family in which every member, from grandmother to the baby, has some share in the orchestra, adds one strand to the harmony. The baby can come in with the rattle and the goo-goo.

I have known such households. One boy would play the flute, another the violin, a third the cornet or clarinet. One girl would preside at the piano, a second at the apollo-harp, while a third fingered the guitar or the banjo. To be sure, it might be necessary in most cases to call in a neighbor or two, not all fathers having so many arrows in their quivers. In that case, call it a neighborhood orchestra, and play with all the more animation.

We are very careless in this matter, we parents. We take it for granted that every child must learn the piano, if she is a girl, or the violin, if he is a boy. We take no thought for the family enjoyment, but only for the possible chance to show off in some one else's parlor. There is only one piano at home, and that, with the exception of an occasional duet, accommodates but one performer at a time. The social side of music is lost in the egotistic side.

It is just the same with singing. Let your two boys learn to sing both base and tenor— though some low notes or some high notes must occasionally be sung an octave away from their proper places; and let your two girls sing alto and soprano. Pitch in, yourself, wherever it seems weak! How much better that is than for Susie alone to chase her tra-la-la's up and down the scale, while the rest of the family are bored.

The value of music as a softener and sweetener of home life is inestimable. The home is enriched with a multiplicity of interests, continually varying. Its powers of self-entertainment and of entertaining others are enormously increased. Minds are quickened, hearts are made more happy, differences of temper are merged in the flood of melody. Old and young are knit together, and the saloon and ballroom would have no attractions for the young folks of such a household.

These advantages have been so beautifully set forth by the music-loving poet, Sidney Lanier, that I can do no better than quote his eloquent words: "Given the raw material,—to wit, wife, children, a friend or two, and a house,—two other things are necessary. These are a good fire and music. And inasmuch as we can do without the fire for half the year, I may say that music is the one essential. After an evening spent around the piano or the flute or the violin, how warm and how chastened is the kiss with which the family all say good-night! Ah, the music has taken all the day's cares and thrown them into its alembic, and boiled them and rocked them and cooled them till they are crystallized into one care, which is a most sweet and rare and desirable sorrow—the yearning for God. We all, from little daughter to father, go to bed with so much of heaven in our hearts, at least, that we long for it unutterably, and believe it."

## CHAPTER XXVIII.

SOME HINTS FOR ENTERTAINERS.

IT is a blessed art, this art of entertaining guests, and certainly one has hardly learned "how to play" till he has learned how to set others to playing. Some are "natural entertainers," but the most of us, being naturally selfish, find that at first we are awkward and unsuccessful hosts. Let no one despair. Some of the most delightful of entertainers have risen to that beautiful supremacy after many a determined struggle with bashfulness and coldness and general boorishness. If entertaining "comes hard" to you, rub in the oil of brotherly kindness until it "comes easy."

I count the very first essential to the success of any party that the hostess enjoy it herself. If she is having a good time, the contagion will reach her guests, no matter though the kitchen stove smokes and the ice-cream fails to arrive. On the other hand, if she is hurried and anxious, though the reason for her trepidation may be entirely hidden, the emotion itself cannot be hidden, but every guest is under a constraint, and the evening is spoiled, perhaps no one knows just why.

Napoleon got to going into battle with a certain prestige and assurance of victory that was in itself half the fight. An experienced hostess has gained this Napoleonic confidence, and her manifest ease puts at ease every one that enters her portals. You may be awkward at first and make many blunders, but with each party you give in the right spirit some of this awkwardness will wear away, until at length you will have become yourself a Napoleon of good cheer. Your party will not then be an occasion of dread, but of happy inspiration and of nothing but joyful memories for all.

A party is already far on its way toward success if the guests are well chosen. The wise beginner in entertaining will invite only two or three, and will increase the number of her guests only as her resources in the entertainer's art have increased. There is a natural limit also, since some will never get beyond the three-guest ability or the four-guest ability, just as some teachers that are glorious with small classes are failures with large ones, and some men that make capital sergeants would make a mess of it as colonels.

Much depends also, as may well be understood, on selecting congenial guests. Do not make the mistake, however, of thinking that all must be in the same "set." One of the chief pleasures of social assemblies is in the discovery of delightful folks you had not known before, the introduction of people that should know each other, but do not. Always plan this element of surprise for your parties.

And especially, if you want to get the highest enjoyment from your party, invite at least one person out of pure kindness—some one that is not attractive to you, nor very congenial, it may be, to any one, but needs to be helped in ways in which the occasion may be made to help. If you can feel that your party has transplanted a wall flower to the centre of the garden, or coaxed forth the concealed beauties of some lovely soul hidden back of an ugly husk, you will have reaped the noblest reward your entertainment has to give.

Do not make up your list of guests just to "pay off debts." While of course one or two may be included for this reason that might not otherwise be included, for you to bring together to one house a motley company of folks just because you have been to their separate houses is the extreme of social absurdity, and only a miracle could produce a pleasant evening for guests so fortuitously gathered.

Next, if you would succeed in your entertainment, you must have a good programme. It must be definite, and it is best written down. It must be comprehensive, including all the details of the evening. And it must be generous, since it is always better to have plans for more than the time than to fall short of amusement, and find yourself and guests suddenly face to face with a horrible, unforeseen blank.

In planning for the evening's fun never have in mind the showing off of yourself or of any one or anything. The question is not at all what entertainment best pleases you and what games you are a success in, but what your guests will enjoy. If they are not skilled in rhyming, do not embarrass them with crambo, though crambo may be your especial delight. If they are mentally bright do not hesitate to propose crambo, though ·you never could rhyme, and crambo is your pet aversion. In entertaining, as in everything else, to find your life you must lose it.

The first point in the programme is to provide something to "break the ice," something to occupy the often awkward moments while the guests are arriving and no game can be begun. Something to look at is most useful here—a lot of somethings, about which the guests may group themselves, passing them from hand to hand, drawing newcomers to them with bursts of delight, and getting acquainted over them in spite of themselves. You may have to borrow this initial feature. It may require the combination of several households; and you may need for the sake of these opening minutes to ask some friend to come in and help you entertain. If so, all the better.

From this point as a basis, the programme should be built up with short alternations of light amusements and heavy amusements, mental and physical. First, perhaps, some action game to fuse the company together. Next, some quiet game with pencil and paper. Thus you will pass from one type of amusement to another, and in this variation the evening will pass before any one realizes it.

For a sample programme, this: Several tables are heaped with photographs brought there by your brother's friend, Will Holcomb, who is an enthusiastic amateur photographer and has just returned from a long journey with his camera. The photographs are all named on the back, but Will is there with his bright and eager explanations. The guests having arrived, they are set to hunting for a hidden paper—a game described elsewhere in this book. After all eyes have made the important discovery, a round or two of dumb crambo serves still further to organize the company. The more sedate "spello" follows; then the hilarious egg football. While all are gathered laughing around the table, and begging for just one more try at it, various dishes of candy, cakes, fruit, and nuts are placed before them, and all are bidden to fall to just where they are sitting. The evening closes with a "sing" out of the delightful Franklin Square song-books.

Not that something to eat is necessary. Many a party has been spoiled by over-attention to the stomach. The hostess was in the parlor, but her mind was evidently in the kitchen. All the entertainment was plainly a mere preliminary to the ice-cream and charlotte russe, and after that formidable part of the evening's exercises was over without smashing a dish or spilling a spoonful, the air of the hostess has said as plainly as words, "Now you may go home. You have had it!"

Do not think that you cannot give a party without something to eat. Some of the most successful evening's entertainments, forever fragrant in my memory, never heard the clatter of a plate, and never even thought of the œsophagus. If you do introduce the gustatory element, let it enter as a by-the-way, without heralding, with no awkward pause in the fun, without arranging the company in the stiff wall-flower ranks so familiar to all of us; manage to bring it in so skilfully that the current of gaiety may ripple smoothly over it and not be dammed up by a frigid wall of orange sherbet.

Indeed, this quality of smoothness, this easy flow of the entertainment, is the chief test and proof of an experienced hostess. It can come only as the affair is well planned, and all its details are securely held in mind; only, too, as every member of the family, from grandfather to little Bobby, helps in the execution of the plans, each having a part to play, and knowing just how to do it. One person that is good at entertaining is a host, but a whole family of such persons is irresistible.

I should have spoken of the welcome, of the necessity that the hostess should be near the door, that her voice should be cordial, her hand and heart both warm. Nothing is more important than these first words of greeting. Nothing, that is, except the good-byes, for those place upon the evening its final stamp and seal. Keep up the brightness to the end. Many an otherwise delightful entertainer stiffens out when she comes to dismiss her guests, and does not seem to know how to do it.

There is a radiant smile, there is a sincere ring to the voice, there is a manifest overflowing of friendship which may grace these farewells, and which will follow the guests out into the street, and go home with them, and glow through their dreams, and float like a halo above every thought of the evening's enjoyment. "Good-bye!" Never forget that that means, "God be with you!"

## CHAPTER XXIX.

YOUR OWN GAMES.

SINCE the world began, how many forms of work have been invented, and how few modes of play! How many poems have been made, and how few games! The game is as truly a work of art as a poem, and what poem, even of the masters, has done as much good in the world as a good game? Yet laurels for the poet's brow, while the game-inventor sleeps in an unknown grave!

Not that there are not in the aggregate many noble games; but in proportion to his activity in other and less important directions, man has left this line of effort with strangely little attention. The patent office turns out every year hundreds of new games which allure our children with gaudy colors and attractive names; but what poor trash they are! Even the fun-loving, easily-pleased children soon weary of them, and no wonder. Most of them are the emptiest of imitations. Nearly all the card games are merely "Authors" disguised. The board games are nearly all made upon one and the same principle. "Pigs in Clover" appears, and at once becomes the ancestor of whole litters of puzzles. Crokinole introduces a bright new method, and straightway the circular disk becomes the basis of a swarm of games, with a most suspicious family resemblance. There is an evident lack of originality in this field of game-invention.

And why? Because we do not try to invent games. The children do. Every child is his own game-inventor, and asks no favors from the patent office. A box of spools is dumped upon the floor, and lo, a fascinating game! A pile of clothespins is discovered on the grass, and behold game number two! The child looks at things with originality and with fun-loving eyes, and those two factors always bring forth games.

It was thus, I fancy, that all good games were invented. A friend of mine was fond of letter games. He and his wife laid their letters down, taking turns, upon a chess board, and thus spelled words, and the delightful game of Klova was born. A man was snapping buttons with his little girl, and straightway Tiddledy-winks was thought of. Another man was reading about the cowboys, and there sprung into his game-ready mind that excellent sport, all-too-short-lived—Lassola. I myself am fond of inventing games, some of which have proved their worth by getting themselves paid for; and the rule is, always start with whatever comes to hand, with whatever your eye or your mind lights upon, and then—play with it. That is the way the children do.

There are many gains from this habit—for it is a habit—of game-inventing. The chief advantage is that it lifts you to the level of the child; you become bright enough to play with children!

Another gain is that you yourself, if no one else, will get vast enjoyment from these games of yours. They may be poor games, but ah, they are your own!

And for a third gain, why not patent them? If they are worth playing, we will all buy them, never fear; and we won't grudge you a cent of your profits.

## CHAPTER XXX.

#### A GAME REPERTOIRE.

FEW greater blessings can come to this overworked age than a sane, pure, jolly game. In this century we need to echo Sancho Panza's "God bless the man who first invented sleep!" and add a further blessing on the man that invents a good game.

But those that recognize the high moral and physical—yes, and spiritual—blessing of a proper game, are often astonished to observe how few have learned the best games. One of the most pitiful things about the playgrounds for city children is that the poor little waifs, when let loose in their new playgrounds, are at a loss what to do. They have never learned how to play, and a teacher of games has at once to be provided. I do not believe that such teachers are easy to find, for most of us grown-ups are in the sad condition of the street children.

Every Christian that is bent on making his life as bright and sunny as possible will store his memory with a plentiful supply of games, and will put his cheery knowledge in practice as often as he can.

A game répertoire is not easy to obtain. You must be alert to gather from friends accounts of all bright amusements they may know. Let no allusion to an unfamiliar game pass without full explanation. You must keep your eye on the papers and magazines that make a specialty of reporting the freshest ideas in this important field. You must glean from the odd corners of odd books. After a few years of such study and search, you will find yourself inventing games as good as any of them, and you will become a benefactor of the race.

I have already advised all that have anything to do with the entertainment of friends —and who of us has not?—to keep a little blank book for the purpose of recording these discoveries. Simply the names of the games will usually be enough, but sometimes the rules must be added. Have a division of the book for games that can best be played only by two; another for the games for four; another —and this you will find most useful, and at the same time most difficult to fill—for the games that are suitable for large companies. How often this list will come in play after you have become familiar with it, you cannot, without trying it, have any idea.

"Life is real, life is earnest." No one feels this more deeply than I do. No one is more anxious, young people, that you should make the most of it, for the sake of the One who gave it. But for that very reason I am an advocate of healthy amusement, because without it you will not—you cannot—make the most of life, and the most of the powers of body, mind, and spirit, that God has given you. It is for His sake, and to be used in His service, that I urge you to get a répertoire of games.

It may well be thought that this book should contain at least the outline of such a répertoire. I have attempted to supply it in the following lists, for which I am sure my readers will come to thank me more than for any other portion of this volume. My limitations of space have compelled the most extreme brevity, so that I may be pardoned for a reference here to two of my books in which all these games are fully described, together with many others: "Social Evenings" and "Social to Save," both published by the publishers of this book. In those volumes I have also given full directions for scores of "socials," or entire evening's entertainments for large parties, and I have made no attempt to condense here any of these more extended schemes.

The following list does not include, either,

that large class of games suitable only to special holidays, such as the games that have grown up around Christmas or Halloween. There are numerous books, such as "The Book of Days," which supply full information concerning these interesting but restricted games. The list that follows is one suited to all times and seasons.

Doubtless every reader will glance with amusement, if not with disgust, at some of the paragraphs below, saying, " Why has he filled up his space with that commonplace game which I have known since I was a baby?" Doubtless, too, these scorned paragraphs will be in each case an entirely different set, since the games with which one person or one section of the country is familiar are often entire strangers and most welcome acquaintances to many others. My only fear is that in taking it for granted that every one knows about some capital old game like "Clumps," I have been a faithless master of ceremonies and left some noble veterans to stand awkwardly as wall flowers.

First in the catalogue shall stand

### ACTION GAMES.

Games that require bodily activity, that call in play the muscles, make the eye keener, the hand readier, the feet more prompt, have a decided value in themselves. They have a value for the mind, rendering it more alert, and they have an immediate value for the spirit, freshening it and invigorating it as more intellectual games may not be able to. Besides, these action games are most useful to intersperse among more sedate and arduous amusements, and serve admirably to lighten an evening's entertainment.

The list that follows is, of course, far from complete, but it is representative and I hope suggestive, and will constitute a good nucleus to which your own observation and invention may add.

*Dumb Crambo.*—Divide the company into halves. One half thinks of a word, say "quay," and tells the other group that it rhymes with "tree." Group number two must proceed to act out words rhyming with "tree" till they light on "quay." Group number one must guess each time what word group number two is acting.

*Ruth and Jacob.*—Form a ring, putting a man and a woman in the centre. Blindfold "Ruth." "Where art thou, Jacob?" she must cry. He answers promptly, "Here am I, Ruth," at the same time dodging her. When he is caught, he is blindfolded and chooses a new Ruth, whom he catches, and thus the game alternates.

*Bookbinding.*—Each player sits with closed hands extended, knuckles up, a book resting across. The bookbinder must snatch a book and rap the knuckles before the owner of the latter draws them back. If he succeeds in this, or if he merely pretends to snatch the book and the holder lets it fall, the victim becomes bookbinder.

*Meal-Bag Races.*—Tie the contestants in stout sacks, their heads alone out, and let them race across the room.

*Three-Legged Race.*—Tie your contestants in pairs, the right leg of one to the left leg of his partner, and let the pairs race.

*Spin the Platter.*—Number the company, and seat them in a circle. One player spins a plate on the floor, at the same time calling a number, whose owner must catch the plate before it falls. If he fails, he becomes spinner.

*Bringing It Down.*—Hang a bag of candy from the ceiling by a string, and let the players take turns in advancing toward (?) it blindfolded and trying to hit the bag with a cane, thus scattering its contents for a scramble.

*Egg Football.*—At each end of a table set up two saltcellars as goal posts. Appoint two players as goal-keepers, and arrange their sides so that they will alternate down the table. A blown egg is the football, and it is to be moved solely by blowing against it. If it falls, put it back where it fell off.

*Porca, or Italian Blindman's Buff.*—Form a circle, which moves several times around a blindfolded player in the centre. He touches a player with a stick, which the player must seize. He then grunts like a pig, or makes some other animal noise, which the player must imitate as closely as possible. When the blindfolded player guesses who holds the other end of his stick, that person takes his place in the centre.

*Clothespins.*—The opposing sides stand in rows facing each other, and see who can first pass a pile of clothespins down the row to a chair and then back to a chair at the head of the row. The piles contain equal numbers of pins. The pins may be transferred from player to player one at a time, or all at once. A dropped pin must be picked up before the bundle can be passed on.

*The Hidden Paper.*—Hunt for a piece of white paper two inches square placed in plain view. The players seat themselves as each discovers the paper.

*Spoons.*—Blindfold two players and seat them on the floor. They are to feed each other cracker crumbs or bananas with spoons. Each player may also be required to feed himself water with a spoon, holding the spoon by the extreme end.

*The Runaway Feather.*—The players hold a sheet at the level of their mouths, stretching it tight, and blow from one to another a bright-colored feather which a player standing outside the circle tries to catch. The player nearest whom he catches it takes his place.

*Dumb Band.*—Each player acts out in pantomime the playing of some instrument, in time to a brisk tune on the piano. The leader plays an imaginary violin, but changes rapidly to the different instruments, and as he changes, each player in turn must take up the violin, on penalty of a forfeit.

*Peanut Race.*—This is harder than the better known potato race. Each contestant must transfer a pile of peanuts from one plate to another at the other side of the room, taking them as many at a time as he can carry them upon a table knife. The victor is the one who transports the largest number of nuts within the time set.

*Cobwebs.*—Threads of different colors are wound intricately about the room. Each player, choosing a badge of a certain color, must find the end of the thread of that color, and wind the thread upon a spool, the victor being the one who first completes his task.

*Three Deep.*—Arrange the players in two circles, one within the other, each player on the inside standing just in front of one on the outside. One player remains out and pursues another, who may stop on the outside of the circle at any point. When this happens, and the circle thus becomes three deep, the inside player leaps to the outside (or he may be caught) and is pursued in his turn, until *he* chooses to make the circle three deep. When any player is caught, he becomes pursuer, and the person who caught him becomes the pursued.

*Needles and Thread.*—This is a contest for the young men, who are to see which one can first string ten needles upon a thread, tying a knot after each needle.

*Number Groups.*—Each person is given a card bearing a number. The leader chooses some large number and calls it out. The players strive to form sets the united numbers on whose cards equal the sum announced, and the first complete group to present itself to the leader is victorious, each member of the group receiving a slip of red paper. After several rounds of this, the person with the most red slips is declared the winner.

*Throw the Handkerchief.*—Knot a handkerchief and throw it from one side to the other of a circle of players, one player in the centre trying to get possession of it. If he succeeds, the person that threw it must take his place.

Other action games, such as "Do you know Uncle Ned?" "Feathers," "Hunt the Slipper," "Going to Jerusalem," "Hunt the Ring," "Magic Music," and "Up Jenkins," might be added to the list, but they are probably well known to all my readers, and I can pass on to give a list of

PENCIL AND PAPER GAMES.

*Adjective Stories.*—Some one writes a comical story, with many personal allusions, leaving frequent blanks for adjectives, which are supplied hit-or-miss by the members of the company, each giving one. The story, thus completed, is then read.

*Psychology.*—The leader announces a word, say "Boston," and for five or ten minutes each player makes a list of the successive suggestions that come spontaneously to mind; that is, "Boston" might suggest "baked beans," and that might suggest "oven," and that "oven bird," and so on. All the lists are read slowly by the leader, the company guessing the various authors.

*Sonnets.*—Give out one by one the terminal words of a sonnet. Each player must fill out the lines, as they are given, with the proper ten syllables, the productions then being read aloud.

*Telegram.*—A set of ten letters is fixed upon at random, and each player writes an imaginary telegram whose words begin, in order, with these ten letters.

*Illustrated Proverbs.*—Each person present makes a drawing illustrating some proverb he has in mind. These drawings are passed around, and the players write their guesses as to the proverb intended, the guesses being folded over so as to be concealed until the close of the game, when they are read aloud.

*Illustrated Quotations.*—The same, using common quotations.

*Novels.*—This is played like "consequences," only the players first write at the head of their slips of paper the title of a story, real or imaginary, fold the paper so as to hide what they have written, pass and write the name of some author, then in the same way a name of a hero, one of a heroine, a brief synopsis of the plot of the unknown book, and finally a brief review of it, after which the papers are opened up and read.

*Doubles.*—Choose sides and see, for instance,

which side can change "head" to "tail" in the fewest moves, the winning side to choose one member from the other side. The solution might be: "Head, heal, teal, tell, tall, tail." Next you might change a "wren" to a "hawk," etc.

*Composite Pictures.*—Each player draws on the upper third of a piece of paper the head of some animal. Fold this under, leaving merely the ends of the necks visible, and then pass. Next the bodies are to be drawn, and finally the legs. Then open the papers, and behold! a new zoology.

*Nouns and Adjectives.*—Give each player a letter of the alphabet and ask him to write on a piece of paper a noun and an adjective beginning with his letter. Distribute these slips at random. Each player must then draw a picture illustrating what has been assigned him. If "chair, cowardly" is the prescription, for instance, draw a girl standing on a chair, looking at a mouse.

*Outlines.*—Provide the players with cards upon which is drawn the same irregular line, which each player must then incorporate in the picture of some animal or person.

*Alliteration.*—See who can write the longest story on a given subject, using words beginning with the same letter. Or draw letters by lot and let each write a sentence whose words all begin with the letter he has drawn.

*Rhapsodies.*—The company will make up a list of words, of all parts of speech, and will then set themselves to incorporating these words in stories in the order in which they are given. Limit the stories in length.

*Spello.*—Choose a word with a great variety of vowels and consonants, and see who can make the most words beginning with the first letter and containing no letters not found in the model word, doubling only the letters found doubled therein. Each word of your list will count for you as many points as there are persons that did *not* think of that word, multiplied by the number of syllables in the word. Go on to the other letters in order, and at the close sum up your counts.

*Transpositions.*—Each player chooses from a set of letters the letters that make up the name of some famous person or place, and passes the set around the circle, accompanied with a brief written description giving a good hint in regard to the proper name chosen. The victor is the one that solves, within the time assigned for examination, the largest number of these puzzles.

*Alphabet Stories.*—Set the company to writing little stories of twenty-six words that begin with the letters of the alphabet taken in order.

*What Would You Do If?*—Number the company and ask each to write a question beginning: "What would you do if—" such or such a thing should happen. Collect these and re-number. They will next write, using their new numbers, an independent answer: "I should-——." Collect and distribute by chance, a question and answer to each. Let the questions be read in order, and after each the answer that has the same number.

*Capping Verses.*—Each person present writes in a vertical column a set of rhyming words, and hands it to his neighbor, who must fill it out, forming a stanza.

*Cento Verses.*—Each player writes a line of poetry, passes the paper, and his neighbor must write a line rhyming with the first. So it goes on as far as is desired.

*Advice Gratis.*—Write a large number of pieces of witty advice. Each member of the company must draw one and read it aloud, solemnly stating before he looks at it whether it is good advice or bad.

*Noted Men.*—The players make lists of famous men whose names begin with A, and when the allotted time has expired, each reads his list. Each name counts for him as many points as there are persons that have not written it down.

*Blank Proverbs.*—One player of a small group thinks of a proverb or familiar quotation, and writes a line of dots separated by vertical lines, to represent the letters and the words. The other players call for a letter—say " e "—and he inserts it wherever it belongs. So with other letters, till the proverb is guessed. If, however, the proverb is not guessed by the time *three* letters that are *not* in it have been called for, the propounder of the puzzle is victorious.

There are many other writing and drawing games, such as "Crambo," and "Consequences," that are too well known to need description. We can go on to games that do not require paper and pencils or anything but a quick brain, and which, therefore, I have called

### GAMES OF WIT.

*City Chains.*—Two groups of players face each other, and one group names a city. Before the umpire has measured off a quarter of a minute the other group must name a city beginning with the *last* letter of the first-named city, and so it goes till one side fails and loses a member to the other side, when a new chain is started.

*Lawyer.*—Each person playing chooses a lawyer. One stands in the centre and asks questions of the different players in as natural and brisk a way as possible. No one must reply, on penalty of a forfeit, but his lawyer, on the same penalty, must at once reply for him. If he fails, he takes the questioner's place.

*Proverbs.*—Doubtless well known. A player is sent from the room, and the words of a proverb are assigned to the members of the company, in order. The player returns and asks questions of the others, each reply to introduce the assigned word till the proverb is guessed.

*Shouting Proverbs.*—This is like the above, except that when the player returns to the room, on a given signal every person *shouts* his word at the top of his voice, and this is kept up till the proverb has been guessed.

*Matched Proverbs.*—Choose sides. One side thinks of a proverb and tells its leading word. If the other side cannot name the proverb, they lose a member. On the contrary, they gain one from the other side for every proverb they can name that contains the word proposed.

*Snap Proverbs.*—Send one player out and arrange the rest in a row, giving each a word of a proverb. The player returns and asks the first player his word. When it is given, he at once turns to another player and requires him to name five—minerals, artists, cities, whatever he pleases—that begin with the same initial. If the player succeeds before the leader counts thirty, he goes to the head of the line. If he fails, he goes to the foot.

*Acted Proverbs.*—Played like charades, except that a proverb is the theme, and there is usually only one scene.

*Pro and Con.*—The players face one another in two lines. The first on one side gives a word beginning with "pro," and his antagonist must give one beginning with "con" before the umpire counts ten, or, failing, leaves the ranks. Thus it goes on till only one is left. No word may be given twice.

*Theatrical Adjectives.*—One player retires, and in his absence the others hit on an adjective. On his return he asks questions, and the company will answer in the manner prescribed by the adjective, that is, for instance, in a "lazy" fashion, or a "brisk" fashion, or an "indignant" way. The person whose action gives the guesser his clue takes his place.

*Definitions.*—One player thinks of a word, as, "tree," and tells a word with which it rhymes, as, "bee." The other must try to guess the word, but instead of asking, "Is it 'sea'?" etc., they must use definitions, and ask, "Is it a very large body of water?" and the leader must reply, "No, it is not a sea." Thus proceed till the word is guessed, the guesser then propounding a new word.

*Who Are You?*—A player leaves the room and a historical character is chosen. On his return he is bombarded with questions addressed to him as if he were the person thought of, this being continued till he has guessed who he is.

*Who Am I?*—In this game one player chooses his character, and acts it out till the rest of the company have guessed it.

*Progressive Spelling.*—Put the players in a row. The first thinks of a word and tells its first letter. He thinks of "cat," we will say, and gives "C." "H," adds his neighbor, thinking of "chair." "I," continues the third player, thinking of "chisel." "C," says the fourth, thinking of chicken." "A," adds the fifth, having in mind "chicanery." If any one fails, his neighbor has a turn, and he is dropped from the line unless it turns out that no one is able to add another letter. If, on being challenged, a player is found to have added a letter without having in mind any corresponding word, he is dropped. Continue till one only remains.

*Who Knows That Nose?*—Put half of the company in one room and half in the other, hanging a sheet in the doorway. Through a hole in the sheet one player thrusts his nose, the room in which he stands being dark. If he is not guessed after three guesses, one player is chosen from the other side. If guessed, he goes to the other room, which then takes its turn, darkening its own lights.

*Significant Initials.*—Take turns propounding descriptions of famous people beginning with their initials, such as, "Comical Delineator" (Charles Dickens).

*A Senses Test.*—Fill ten little numbered bottles with substances of various odors, each player being required to smell them and make a list of the substances. Do the same with ten little dishes whose contents must be determined by sight—powdered sugar, white pepper, ground cinnamon, sand, and the like. Ten sounds as different as possible are made simultaneously in a neighboring room, and each must make a list of the ten "instruments" from which the sounds proceed. Let the company file slowly past a table covered with a great variety of things, and then write down as complete a list as possible. Ten substances, disguised to the eye, will then be passed to be tasted. Finally, the room being darkened, ten objects will be passed from hand to hand to be determined by feeling, the names being written when the lights are restored.

*Teapot.*—Banish a player and choose a word of several significations though the same sound. The player returns and asks each of the others a question, to which he replies with a sentence bringing in the word agreed upon, except that the place of the word is to be taken by the word, "teapot." If the word is "pair, pear, pare," and the question, "Have you ever seen a lover?" the answer might be, "Yes, a teapot of them." The person whose reply gives the clue becomes guesser in a new round.

*No-horned Lady.*—The players sit in a circle and one turns to his right-hand neighbor and says, as rapidly as possible, "I, a no-horned lady, always no-horned, come to you, a no-horned lady, always no-horned, to say that this no-horned lady (referring to his left-hand neighbor), always no-horned, has a house with a table (or any other article the speaker may think of) in it." The formula is then passed on, each speaker adding a new article till it becomes a long list. For every mistake made a lamplighter is stuck in the hair, and the unfortunate player becomes a "one-horned lady," a "two-horned lady," etc., and must always be thus described, on penalty of receiving one's self an additional horn.

*Literati.*—One withdraws, and the company think of some famous man, each taking a letter of his name. Returning, the leader questions the player that has the first letter, who replies, having in mind not the person to be guessed, but some historical character beginning with his letter. If Lincoln is to be guessed, he may answer with Lowell in mind; the next player may answer with Isaac in mind, the next thinking of Noah, and so on. Whoever gives the final clue must become guesser in his turn.

*Throwing Light.*—Thinking of a word of several meanings but the same pronunciation, the leader begins to talk about it, speaking of it in its various significations at random, the company interjecting guesses, until some one guesses correctly, and then starts a new puzzle himself.

*What Is It Like?*—A player who has left the room returns to guess some object fixed upon in his absence. "What is it like?" he asks. "Like a door, because it has four corners." "Like our Bridget, because it is green." Thus the answers may run until he discovers the word, "greenback."

*Advertisements.*—Mount upon squares of

pasteboard a series of well-known advertisements, leaving no proper names—nothing but the pictures, "catch" phrases, and the like. Number these, and pass them around for the company to make out a correct list.

*Quotations.*—Arrange the company in two rows facing each other. The leader of one row gives a quotation, and the leader of the opposite row must name the author or pass over to the side of his opponents. The quotations are proposed by each side alternately.

*Catches.*—A book might be written upon these forms of diversion. They are amusing, but a little of them goes a long way. For example, it is proclaimed that Mrs. Brown does not like tea, and it is asked what she *does* like, the players being required to suggest articles of food. If they mention "toast, potatoes, tomatoes," and so on, they are sent indignantly from the circle, but if they name "bread, milk, horseradish," and so on, they are warmly approved, and it will be some time before they discover that Mrs. Brown's aversion is to the *letter* "t."

"Æsop's Museum" is similar, Æsop asking each player what animal he has been eating lately, and permitting him uncondemned to eat any animal provided there is no "o" in its name. Then there are catches of the practical-

## A GAME REPERTOIRE. 155

joke type, like "Farmyard." Each player is given some animal whose characteristic noise he is to make as loudly as possible when the leader's hand is raised, but he is to be silent instantly as soon as the leader's hand is lowered. These instructions are whispered; but the unfortunate person who has to imitate the donkey is not given the latter half of the instructions, so that he innocently and vigorously brays out a solo.

"Pansy" is not unlike this. The leader whispers to each the name of some flower, and says that as each flower is named in the course of a story he will relate, the corresponding player must try to escape from the room before he can be caught. After several narrow escapes the company is all eager attention, sitting on the edges of the chairs. Calmly the story-teller introduces the word, "pansy," whereupon there is a wild rush from the room of everybody but himself. All but two or three had been assigned the same flower.

Forms of "mind-reading," dependent upon some signal given by a comrade, are numerous and puzzling. Perhaps the most obscure is this: Each player writes some word on a piece of paper, which is folded and placed with the others in a box. The mind-reader draws a slip and rubs it mysteriously across his forehead, naming at last some word. His reading is at once confirmed by one of the company, whose word has been agreed upon beforehand, and whose slip is folded in such a way as to be avoided till the last. The mind-reader opens the slip to make sure he is right, and reads, of course, a new word. Taking another slip, he proceeds to draw this word from it by his vast mental powers, much to the mystification of the company. Of course he may do without the accomplice and name first what he himself wrote, having marked his own slip.

My list of games of wit might be largely increased, and I fear I am not safe in taking it for granted that all my readers will know the good old games of "Clumps," "Twenty Questions," "Beast, Bird, and Fish," "How, Where, and When," "Boston," "Traveler's Alphabet," "Steamboat's Coming," "I Love My Love," "Apprentice My Son," and "Buzz." If any of these names is unfamiliar, I advise you to discover its meaning without delay, and straightway practise it!

## LETTER GAMES.

Every household that would be equipped for the long evenings should invest in a twenty-five cent box of cardboard squares, each bearing in bold type a letter of the alphabet. Games in an infinite variety may be played therewith. "Word-making and Word-taking" is well known. Each player draws from the central pile in turn, and builds up ten words which count according to their length, having the option of using the letter he draws to change and thereby capture some word of his antagonists'. "Anagrams" are also well known, each player choosing the letters that form a certain word and passing them to his neighbor, who must write down his solution and pass the letters on.

"Initials" is a delightful game. The first player says to his neighbor: "Name a poet beginning with ——" (The neighbor turns over one of his letters and quickly announces) "T." If he gets out his "Tennyson" before any one else shouts his "Tupper," he retains the card; otherwise, it goes to the more prompt player. Next the name of some general may be called for, or of some kind of cloth, or some plant, or —anything.

Some romp games of letters are these. Throw the letters in a heap, face up, and see who first can pick out from the heap a complete alphabet, laying down A first, then B, etc., and all working at once. Then go on to a simultaneous picking out of *words*, the "rush" to continue as long as any letters remain, and the victor to be the person whose count is the highest, a one-syllabled word counting two, a two-syllabled word four, a three-syllabled word six, and so on.

### BIBLE GAMES.

The largest publisher of games in the country once told me that no games sell better than those based on the Bible. You may make them for yourself. For instance, "Bible Salad," which consists of a dish full of Bible "leaves," on each of which is written some verse from the Bible, the slips being numbered consecutively. As the players draw the slips and read them aloud, all are required to write, opposite the proper number, the name of the Bible book from which the quotation is taken. Questions about the Bible may be written on slips of paper and used in much the same way. The publishers of this book publish some excellent Bible games.

### CARD GAMES.

It is of slight value to give a list of these, since a good game will have vogue, and be found everywhere in the stores, and then go out of fashion mysteriously and be obtainable nowhere. I have in mind several games which became favorites in my household. We gave away our copies, and since then have been unable to replace them.

Most of these card games are based upon that pioneer in this important field, "Authors," and like it aim to combine fun and instruction; so that there are few subjects, from oak-trees to art, from kings and queens to common fractions, from battleships to orthoepy, that may not be pleasantly studied through this medium.

Until the publishing and selling of card games has passed out of its present vague and fluctuating condition and reached the stage of catalogues and permanency, any list of these games, in a volume intended for more than the present year, would be nothing but a source of perplexity and disappointment.

### BOARD GAMES.

These are more permanent than card games, but the really good ones are few in number and are almost universally known. By good ones I mean those that do not depend wholly upon luck, upon the whirl of a disk, the shaking of dice, or the revolution of a pointing arrow, that sends "men" to various intricate destinations absurdly up and down a gaudily colored board. Of course there is a gradual gradation from the board games that are purely games of chance to those that are wholly games of skill. "Parchesi" is along this line of transition, and I remember many pleasant hours spent over the game. Backgammon, with its even more fascinating variation, Russian backgammon, calls also for a certain measure of thought. Thence one goes up the scale to such fine and altogether admirable amusements as "Klova," "Archarena," "Halma," "Carroms," "Crokinole," "Checkers," not forgetting one of my favorites, "Pyramid Checkers," nor omitting, either, "Fox and Geese," "Spider," "Bob," and "Tiddledy-winks," and so up the delightful line till we reach the sparkling climax, "Chess"!

There are many other games worthy of mention here, but hard to classify—take "Pillow Dex" as a sample. And besides, there is a whole world of

OUTDOOR GAMES

known only to the happy school children, but well worth knowing by some of us unfortunates that have forgotten our school days —games such as "Wolf," "Still Pond," "Widow," "Red and Black," "Wood Tag,"

"Hop-Scotch," and "Anthony Over." We are so silly, running after fads, in these outdoor sports under the free sky, where a fad should hang its head and hide itself. Now it is croquet, and when tennis comes in croquet is forgotten, and when golf arrives, good-bye tennis; archery has its turn, and then basketball; now it is quoits and now it is cricket, with nothing of intelligent choice, and little even of that hearty liking which makes of a game a lifelong friend.

In the wise time coming, when the philosophy of games is better understood and universally practised, all our amusements, outdoors as well as indoors, will be selected, not with a stiff pedantry that will destroy their spontaneity and zest, but with forethought and a sensible appreciation of their different characteristics and what they will do for one. Certainly it is not true that for all the world —old and young, active and sedative, phlegmatic and ardent, quick and sluggish—the best game this year is golf, any more than it will be true of them all next year that the best game is lacrosse or polo. Men are not built on the same pattern, nor do they vary simultaneously. Play all "likely" games, till you find what games you like and what like you. Then adhere to them with the tenacity of a true lover, though they grow as unpopular as croquet. The proverb names three things that are best old—old wine, old books, and old friends; "three things, nay, four," we may say, and add, "old games."

# Our Latest Publications.

## Lincoln at Work. By William O. Stoddard.

Finely illustrated by Sears Gallagher. 173 pages, cloth, embellished cover design. Price, $1.00.

Probably no one is better acquainted with the every-day life of Abraham Lincoln than William O. Stoddard, one of his secretaries at the White House during the greater part of the war. In a series of fascinating and most graphic chapters, Colonel Stoddard pictures the gaunt, ungainly young politician, his rapid and marvellous rise to power, and that strange life in the White House, so appealing in its pathos, its quaint humor, and the profound tragedy that lay underneath it all. The author makes us feel as if we ourselves had been permitted to sit by the side of the great President in his dark workroom, or to be present at his momentous and striking conferences with his generals. Many anecdotes are told, throwing a flood of light upon the times and the man, and the whole closes with a powerful picture of the impression produced by Mr. Lincoln's death, even in the South, where Colonel Stoddard was at the time. Mr. Stoddard is an accomplished story-writer as well as a skilful historian, and both qualities come into play in making this delightful and important book.

## From Life to Life. By Rev. J. Wilbur Chapman, D. D.

200 pages, cloth. Price, $1.00.

A collection of anecdotes, stories, incidents, poems, and other illustrative material drawn from many sources and touching many topics. A leading feature of the book is the large number of incidents taken from life and carrying their own lessons. The compiler, well known as one of the foremost evangelists, gathered the matter for his own use from his own observation; and the choicest parts have been selected for this volume. It will therefore be of great interest and value to Christian workers generally, whether for their own help or as an aid in winning others.

## Doings in Derryville. By Lewis V. Price.

212 pages, cloth, 60 cents; paper, 25 cents.

This story is of a noble young girl who finds herself in one of those many country towns which have quite lost their Christianity and become almost pagan. The church was closed, Sunday was a lost day, worldliness and Satan had full control.

In a series of wide-awake and stirring chapters, Mr. Price describes the organization of a Christian Endeavor society. A Sunday school soon follows, and later comes a pastor, who is willing to use his powers in meeting the great need, and for love of his country and God do what he can to build up the neglected country town. The incidents woven into the story are all actual facts which have come under the author's own observation. Two beautiful love stories sweeten the tale and add to its human interest.

---

**UNITED SOCIETY OF CHRISTIAN ENDEAVOR,**
Boston and Chicago.

# The Deeper Life Series.

*A series of daintily bound books upon spiritual themes by the leading religious writers of the age. Bound in uniform cloth binding. 6 3-4 by 4 1-2 inches in size. Price, 35 cents each.*

## The Inner Life. By Bishop John H. Vincent, D. D.

"A study in Christian experience" which shows how the life of the soul is the true reality, and what striking results are wrought when the power of Christ and the indwelling of the Holy Spirit become the controlling forces in a life.

## The Loom of Life. By Rev. F. N. Peloubet, D. D.

"The threads our hands in blindness spin,
Our self-determined plan weaves in."

"The Loom of Life," and "If Christ were a Guest in our Home," which is also included in this volume, are two very helpful sketches by the author of that well-known publication, Peloubet's "Select Notes." Many new and forceful truths are presented, such as will give the reader thought for serious consideration for many a day. The book abounds in apt illustrations and anecdotes, in the use of which Dr. Peloubet is so skilful.

## The Improvement of Perfection.
By Rev. William E. Barton, D. D.

This is not a treatise on the higher life, but is meant to help young Christians to a higher life by showing what kind of perfection God expects, and how it is to be gained, at the same time furnishing an incentive to attain it. The aim is practical rather than theoretical, and the style is clear and attractive.

## I Promise. By Rev. F. B. Meyer.

The book is appropriately called "I promise." Its chapters deal with matters of the utmost importance to every Christian, such themes as "Salvation and Trust," "Winning God's Attention," and "What Would Jesus Do?" In strong, sensible, winsome words the path of duty is pointed out, and conscience is spurred to follow it.

**UNITED SOCIETY OF CHRISTIAN ENDEAVOR,**
Boston and Chicago.

# The "How" Series.

## By AMOS R. WELLS.

*7 1-4 by 4 1-2 inches in size. Uniformly bound in cloth with illuminated cover design. About 150 pages each. Price, 75 cents each.*

## How To Work.

This is a working nation, and yet few among its millions of workers know how to work to the best advantage and with the best results. The fundamental principles of wise labor are set forth in these chapters in a familiar, conversational style. Much of the book consists of actual talks given to young men and women starting out in life. "Puttering," "Putting Off," "Hurry Up!" "Taking Hints," "A Pride in Your Work," "'Can' Conquers," "The Bulldog Grip," "The Trivial Round,"—these are specimen titles of the thirty-one chapters. The book is not didactic, but presents truth in illustrations, so that it *sticks*.

## How To Play.

The author of this book evidently believes in recreation. The very first chapter is entitled, "The Duty of Playing." Separate chapters are devoted to the principal indoor amusements, conversation and reading being the author's preferences, and also to the leading outdoor sports, especially the bicycle and lawn tennis. There are many practical chapters on such themes as how to keep games fresh, inventing games, what true recreation is, and how to use it to the best advantage. "Flabby Playing," "Playing by Proxy," "Fun that Fits," "Overdoing It,"—these are some of the chapter titles. In one section of the book scores of indoor games are described, concisely, but with sufficient fulness.

## How To Study.

These chapters, on a very practical theme, deal with the most practical aspects of it,—such topics as concentration of mind, night study, cramming, memory-training, care of the body, note-taking, and examinations. The author makes full use of his experience as a teacher in the public schools and as a college professor, and the book is largely made up of talks actually given to his students, and found useful in their work. The chapters are enlivened by many illustrations and anecdotes, and the whole is put into very attractive covers.

---

**UNITED SOCIETY OF CHRISTIAN ENDEAVOR,**
Boston and Chicago.

www.ingramcontent.com/pod-product-compliance
Lightning Source LLC
Chambersburg PA
CBHW031354040426
42444CB00005B/287